Herman Melville

Herman Melville

A Biography

MILTON MELTZER

TWENTY-FIRST CENTURY BOOKS
Minneapolis

Photographs courtesy of U. S. Naval Historical Center: pp. 2–3, 71, 76; Peabody Essex Museum, Salem, MA: p. 6; Brown Brothers: pp. 10 (top), 12, 31; New York Public Library: pp. 10 (bottom: Anson Dickinson. Portrait of Maria Gansevoort, 1814. Gansevoort-Lansing Collection, 1650–1919. Manuscripts and Archives Division), 61 (Picture Collection), 65 (Picture Collection), 83 (Typee manuscript, 1845-Page No. 1. Gansevoort-Lansing Collection, 1650–1919. Manuscripts and Archives Division); From *Hudson-Mohawk Genealogical and Family Memoirs*: p. 17 (engraving by A. H. Ritchie, ed. Cuyler Reynolds, vol. 1 (New York, 1911); From *The History of the City of Albany, New York*: p. 19 (by Arthur James Weise/Albany, 1884); Photos12.com/Polaris: p. 22; Lansingburgh Historical Society: p. 25; Image Select/Art Resource, NY: p. 33; Historic Cherry Hill Collections, Albany, NY: p. 36 (*View of the Great Pass on the Helderberg Mountains with the lines of March in service December 1839. Inscribed to the different corps under orders, from drawings at that time by T. Grenell*); © Museum of the City of New York: p. 42; North Wind Picture Archives: pp. 45, 74; Berkshire Athenaeum, Pittsfield, Massachusetts: pp. 47, 63, 68, 86, 88 (both), 92, 100, 116 (both), 117; Private Collection/Bridgeman Art Library: p. 49; Mystic Seaport: p. 52; From Voyages and Travels by G. H. von Langsdorff (London, 1813): p. 58 ("An inhabitant of the Island of Nukahiwa" engraving by J. Storer); © Bettmann/Corbis: p. 105

Text copyright © 2006 by Milton Meltzer

Twenty-First Century Books
A division of Lerner Publishing Group
241 First Avenue North
Minneapolis, MN 55401 U.S.A.

Website address: www.lernerbooks.com

Library of Congress Cataloging-in-Publication Data

Meltzer, Milton, 1915–
    Herman Melville : a biography / by Milton Meltzer.
        v.   cm.
    Includes bibliograpcal references and index.
    Contents: Marvelous adventures — Scars of childhood — Where he wanted to be — Merchant seaman — Dwarfs, not titans — Chasing whales — Tropical paradise — From Tahiti to Honolulu — In the navy — First book — A married man — More children and more books — Writing Moby-Dick — Melville's voice — The years after — "What unlike things".
    ISBN-13: 978–0–7613–2749–3 (lib. bdg.)
    ISBN-10: 0–7613–2749–5 (lib. bdg.)
    1. Melville, Herman, 1819–1891—Juvenile literature. 2. Novelists, American—19th century—Biography—Juvenile literature. [1. Melville, Herman, 1819–1891. 2. Authors, American.] I. Title.
    PS2386 .M38 2006
    813'.3—dc22   2003013694

Manufactured in the United States of America
1 2 3 4 5 6 – BP – 11 10 09 08 07 06

Contents

$\mathcal{T}$he image of Captain Ahab in battle with the ferocious white whale is forever etched in the mind of anyone who has read Melville's greatest masterpiece, Moby-Dick.

---●─✕─●─---

Foreword

When you hear the name Melville it's likely the first thing that pops into your head is *Moby-Dick*. Yes, the title of that novel which is the story of the long and tragic hunt through the world's oceans for the deadly whale called Moby Dick. The whale was enormous—85 feet (26 meters) in length and weighing 80 tons—the largest form of life in nature.

And enormous too is the book. Not so much in the number of its pages, for there are many novels that are even longer. But in the magnitude of its achievement. It was a new and daring thing for young Melville—or any American writer—to attempt. He was only thirty when he wrote what is now valued as a masterpiece of world literature.

Before *Moby-Dick*, Melville wrote books that drew upon his early years as a sailor on trading ships, whalers, and warships. The time he spent on strange islands in the South Pacific earned him a certain celebrity as "the man who lived among cannibals" and sported with beautiful naked girls on tropical beaches. He helped change U.S. practice by his exposure of the cruel practice of flogging sailors. Living with people of various races and classes, he came to conclusions about human nature and character that led him to protest slavery and proclaim equality.

Melville witnessed great changes at home in America, from the struggling years of the young democracy to its rise as a great world power. In his own life he experienced painful change, from an aristocratic beginning to devastating failure and decades of barely scraping by. In between, during some dozen years as an author, he wrote ten books. And then, when *Moby-Dick* failed to please most critics and the public too, he was forced to feed his wife and children by working for nineteen years as a customs inspector on the docks of New York.

When Melville died in 1891, at seventy-two, his passing was hardly noticed. He was all but forgotten until the 1920s, when recognition gradually came as one of America's greatest writers.

Melville spoke of writing as "the art of telling the truth." Not an easy art, but agonizing, emotionally and physically. This book is an attempt to help the reader understand the way Melville lived, and how his experience shaped his work.

Chapter 1

Marvelous Adventures

New York City was Herman Melville's hometown. He was born there on August 1, 1819. "A very promising child," his father said, relieved that the baby had escaped the cholera epidemic ravaging the city. Herman, named after his mother's oldest brother, was the third child of Allan and Maria Gansevoort Melvill (the "e" was added later). Herman's father, a merchant and importer, was a descendant of Scottish nobility.

Another claim to prestige was the fact that grandfather Thomas Melvill had joined the young men at Boston Harbor in 1773 when they boarded the ships of the East India Company and dumped their cargo of tea in the water. He went on to fight in the Battle of Bunker Hill, reaching the rank of major in George Washington's army.

The family of Herman's mother were early settlers from prominent Dutch people. Her father, General Peter Gansevoort, also fought in the American Revolution. The Gansevoorts prospered through land grants in upstate New York and married into the Hudson Valley aristocracy. The two families connected when Allan Melvill met Peter Gansevoort in a business venture and then married Peter's sister Maria.

Allan Melvill began his dry-goods importing business with offices in both Boston and Albany. But in 1818 he decided that New York City was bound to become the commercial

*Herman's parents,
Allan Melvill and his wife,
Maria Gansevoort,
came from prominent families
as evinced by their elegant
attire in these portraits.
Both were painted when
quite young by talented artists
of their time, Allan in
watercolor and Maria in
a charming miniature.*

center of the nation, and moved his business to that thriving port. He set the family up in an elegant house at 6 Pearl Street, facing the tip of Manhattan Island on one side, and on the other, the wharves and shipping offices of the waterfront. The family's standing was so high that the mayor's wife came to welcome them. Soon after Herman's birth the Melvills began to move to socially "better" addresses. By 1828 they were living at 675 Broadway, enjoying the services of housekeeper, cook, nurse, and waiter. The yard the children played in was about the size of a city block.

As Mr. Melvill borrowed money to expand his business, more children were born. There would be four boys and four girls in all. It was a time when many Americans believed there was no limit to prosperity. The young country had begun to expand when President Thomas Jefferson in 1803 bought the vast Louisiana Territory from France for a trifling sum. To get rich quick all you needed was nerve and the ability to raise capital to invest in land or the canals and railroads and factories created by the Industrial Revolution.

But when a financial crisis broke in 1819, life was badly disrupted. It was the first of a long series of crashes that would do great damage to all sectors of the economy. The panic soon became a major depression that would last for years.

Although Mr. Melvill's business was unsteady, Maria was determined to maintain the Gansevoorts' high standing. Not only did the family move into even more expensive homes, but Herman and his older brother Gansevoort were sent to the Columbia Grammar School, attended by children of the "best" families, and then to the New York Male High School.

In his later writings, Herman would recall his childhood in New York's seaport, standing by his father on the wharves, watching the great ships getting under way. His father had often crossed the Atlantic on business. Coming home, he

New York City's lower Broadway was an elegant residential area when the young Melvills settled there to raise their ever-growing family.

would tell his children of the monstrous waves at sea, mountain high; of the masts bending like twigs; and of the cities in France and England he had visited.

Once as a boy, Herman crossed the Hudson by ferry to visit Hoboken in New Jersey and from the height of the Palisades took in the glorious views of New York Harbor.

When Herman was nine, he was taken to Bristol, Rhode Island, for a vacation at the home of his uncle, John D'Wolf. The old sea captain with white hair had long ago sailed to Archangel in Russia. He told of marvelous adventures, such as his journey through Siberia when he had crossed over by land from the Sea of Okhotsk in Asia to St. Petersburg, drawn on a sled by large dogs. It was one of Herman's happiest vacations.

Living not far from City Hall and the Commons, Herman saw the parades and celebrations staged on the Fourth of July. After all, independence from Britain had been gained scarcely fifty years before. Black people too used the Commons for holiday festivals. And when Herman was eight, he must have seen the special New York Emancipation Day Parade of July 5, 1827, which began at City Hall right near the Melvill home and moved down Broadway to the Battery.

About four thousand black marchers, accompanied by several bands, improvising song and dance, flooded through the streets, carrying vivid banners voicing their joy over the final abolition of slavery in New York State. Among the marchers were members of the African marine societies, sailors Melville would one day live and work with—and write about.

Then, in 1830, when Herman was eleven, disaster hit home. Mr. Melvill had entered secretly into a speculative business scheme that went bad. Reluctantly, his wife's rich brother bailed him out. But he soon floundered again. He finally realized he couldn't compete in the New York market. Facing bankruptcy and disgrace, the family decided to seek shelter in Albany, the state capital and the home base of Mrs. Melvill's family, the Gansevoorts.

With his mother and seven brothers and sisters already in Albany, Herman stayed behind to help his desperate father pack the few things he hoped to save from the creditors. His debts still not paid, Mr. Melvill feared he might be arrested at any moment and sent to debtor's prison. They made their way to the dock, to board a boat that would carry them up the Hudson to Albany. It was a flight the boy would never forget. And never again would he enjoy the heedless security of his early childhood.

CHAPTER 2

Scars of Childhood

With all the Melvills present in Albany, the Gansevoort family set them up in a rented house on North Market Street. Herman and his brother Gansevoort were enrolled in the Albany Academy. Herman's courses included reading, spelling, arithmetic, penmanship, grammar, geography, and natural history. There was time for outdoor sports too. Herman made a lifelong friend of a schoolmate named Eli Fly.

But childhood was no longer free and easy for the Melvill boys and girls. Family life was tense, strained by the pressure of a chaotic, uncertain income. For Allan Melvill was no longer a merchant employing others. He was a hired hand, a clerk in a cap and fur store. To made ends meet he was borrowing money from generous relatives, his own and his wife's, sometimes considerable sums. By now they knew there was little prospect that he would ever be able to repay them.

A breath of joy came when Herman won honors from the Albany Academy for top work in his arithmetic class. Awards were handed out in a public ceremony, and when the Albany *Argus* reported the event, it was the first time Herman Melvill saw his name in print. His parents celebrated by taking Herman and his sister Augusta on an eight-hour trip by stagecoach to Pittsfield, a town in the Berkshire hills in western Massachusetts. (Later, Melvill would make the Berkshires his home for many years.)

In September 1831, Herman began his second year at the academy. With the school term barely started, his parents withdrew him and his brothers, Gansevoort and Allan. Small as the tuition was, the family couldn't afford it. It was the end of Herman's formal schooling.

In December of that same year, Herman's father began to act strangely. That he was unwell was plain, but with what? In his Bible, as the new year opened, he marked two verses of Psalm 55: "My heart is sore, pained within me: and the terrors of death have fallen upon me. Fearfulness and trembling are come upon me and horror hath overwhelmed me."

His condition became so manic that family and friends were convinced he was insane. The physicians called in to help could not establish what was wrong. The biographer Hershel Parker wrote: "Allan was raving, as well he might, for he profoundly loved his wife and his children . . . and he was tortured with the knowledge that he had squandered Maria's fortune and his own inheritance. . . ."

On January 28, 1832, he died. He was just short of his fiftieth birthday.

Many small businessmen then, as now, live on a narrow edge. Unless you've experienced it yourself, it's hard to understand what the economic collapse of a family is like. As some who've had that misfortune point out, the real horror is not the loss of luxuries, but the sudden shift in the tone of the people who were once your associates. "Oh him? He's a failure, an ignorant, blind fool. . . ."

It was around this time that Maria Melvill, perhaps trying to give her family a fresh start, added the "e" to their name. It would be Melville from here on out.

A fresh start too in rebuilding the family fortune. Gansevoort, the oldest son, was establishing a business as a furrier, funded by his uncle Peter. Only sixteen, he was now

Upon the death of Herman's father, the Melvill (hereafter to be known as Melville) family's survival depended on the generosity of Maria's brother Peter Gansevoort.

the man of the family. Plunging into the business helped ease grief following the father's death.

Uncle Peter himself launched a new project, the construction of a large modern hotel—the Tremont House—meant to be the best in Albany and to bring him large profits. But tired of having so often shored up his brother-in-law Allan Melvill, he refused to pay the small sums needed to educate Allan's children.

Through Peter's influence, twelve-year-old Herman was given a job at the New York State Bank, earning $150 a year. For the next three years he would walk to work every day, passing boys on their way to school. It must have been painful to lose the promise of education, to give up young dreams of glory. As he would write years later, he learned "to think much and bitterly" before his time. The blighting of hope at so early an age can't be made good, he said. It strikes in "too deep, and leaves such a scar that the air of Paradise might not erase it."

That summer, cholera—the plague devastating New York City—moved on up to Albany. Aware of the terrible suffering it caused, Mrs. Melville rounded up her eight children and rushed them by stagecoach to Pittsfield. There, in the Berkshires, Uncle Thomas Melvill and his family occupied a fine large house and farm. Herman hardly had time to get to know his cousins when Peter Gansevoort wrote to insist that Herman must come right back to his job at the bank, epidemic or no epidemic.

So Herman boarded the stagecoach alone and moved into Uncle Peter's house. Six mornings a week he trudged to the bank, where he dutifully did all they asked of him: copying documents, filing, running errands. It was his first glimpse of wealth, of the many forms its accumulation took—in mortgages, banknotes, promissory notes, bonds, specie. He got to know by sight the men of power who run the world. Not only the bank's directors but the politicians in the state capital they gave favors to and took favors from.

Inside the bank's solid walls he sometimes felt trapped. It was so unlike his childhood down by the docks of Manhattan, with all their pungent smells and raucous sounds and varied sights. Beyond the bank vaults the cholera ravaged Albany. That summer of 1832, a thousand people were infected, and hundreds died, including a cousin of Herman's.

Herman was not a boy who needed a teacher's or a parent's prodding to read. In Uncle Peter's house there were many books, some once belonging to Herman's father. He read much poetry, both English and American, and kept up with the local newspapers and the periodicals from other cities that reached Albany. And of course he exchanged letters with his mother and family in Pittsfield.

Late that summer Herman's grandfather, Thomas Melvill, the Revolutionary War hero, died at eighty-one. His will left nothing to the estate of his now dead son Allan, because his

The elegant walls of the New York State Bank in Albany seemed like a prison to young Herman, who was forced to work there while his family fled to Pittsfield, Massachusetts, to escape from the cholera epidemic.

loans to him had exceeded his portion. And to his son's widow (Herman's mother), he left only $20.

No doubt disappointed by the terms of the will, Mrs. Melville drew cheer from the optimism of her firstborn, Gansevoort. To anyone who knew the seventeen-year-old he seemed a remarkable young man. Extremely self-confident, he was sure he would come out on top, no matter what venture he undertook. He assured his mother that he would make a great success of his business, and she believed him, as she had his father. Still, so little cash was coming in that she now withdrew her daughter Catherine from the Albany Female Academy.

The reduction in living standards must have struck Herman as odd. Almost any of his aunts and uncles could have paid the modest tuition fees the schools asked. Daily in the bank he saw rich and powerful men, several of them related to him, making deals. How could the family connection matter so little to them? Were greed and selfishness ingrained in human nature?

CHAPTER 3

Where He Wanted To Be

Young as Herman was, the bank officers trusted him, occasionally sending him out of town on errands. Once he traveled to Schenectady, his first ride on one of the new railroads. The cars, simply stagecoaches fitted with new wheels to grip the tracks, were pulled by horse or steam engine.

Both Gansevoort and Herman were avid readers. They had access to private or club libraries and borrowed frequently. Popular at that time were the adventurous tales of James Fenimore Cooper, an author the boys' mother had known as a child, when Cooper would drop in at her parents' home. Gansevoort was eager to glean from books what might help him move up in the world. He'd pass on to his younger brother the books he especially liked.

Once, after reading a story by an English writer, Gansevoort concluded that you didn't need a superior mind to make money. He noted in his diary what he probably also discussed with Herman: "To make money it only requires a cool dispassionate disposition joined with talent even below mediocrity; and a determination to sacrifice every inclination and feeling that might come in conflict with it."

In May 1834, assuming Gansevoort's business would continue to thrive, Mrs. Melville moved the family into a new three-story brick house. Only a few days after they settled in, a fire broke out in the business district. Gansevoort's factory,

How exciting it must have been for Herman to be sent on an out-of-town errand on the latest transport invention, the horse-drawn railway car.

where the skins he sold were prepared, was destroyed. It was a shattering loss. Unable to keep on the factory's hired hands, Gansevoort yanked Herman out of his job at the bank and put him to work selling to customers in his store.

Bank clerk, and now store clerk. And this time, with no salary at all. How could his brother pay him when he drew no salary himself? Here was a mother with eight children, their survival dependent on the two oldest, and they were still teenagers.

Somehow Herman scraped together $1.50 to join the Albany Young Men's Association. It was a society that helped boys to help themselves. They debated political issues and social issues, preparing for arguments by reading the recorded opinions of great men, like Edmund Burke, the English orator and statesman, and Henry Clay, the Kentuckian, famous for his speeches in the Senate, and Benjamin Franklin, the philosopher and sage. "The learned are as one man," Herman wrote in a letter to the editor an Albany paper printed, "in their opinion of the importance of debating societies in developing the mind, and prompting to greater and higher efforts."

In the spring of 1835, one of Herman's cousins, Leonard Gansevoort, then about nineteen, surprised the family by running off to the Massachusetts seaport of New Bedford, where he joined the crew of a whaleship. Herman, while still putting in hours at his brother's store, enrolled in the Albany Classical School. A year later, in 1836, he was readmitted to the Albany Academy, studying Latin and literature. He kept his interest in debating alive, joining clubs where he could practice oratory.

Signs of another financial crisis began to appear. Banks had multiplied and expanded in the riskiest way. The boom in canals and railroads had encouraged wild speculation, and when the bubble burst, another great depression gripped the country from which it would not recover fully for some seven years. Businesses collapsed, banks and factories closed. In New York, every third worker was out of a job. Tens of thousands, needy and unable to find work, first ran into debt and then had to be helped somehow, or starve. Nowhere in the rest of the country was life any better.

In April 1837, Gansevoort was forced to file for bankruptcy. His business was ended. At a family council it was decided that Albany was hopeless. Gansevoort, seeking to start another career, would go to New York City to study law in the office of a friend. Herman would go to Pittsfield to run for a while the farm of his uncle Thomas Melvill, who left for Galena, Illinois, in the hope of finding some kind of living out on the undeveloped prairies.

By mid-June, Herman was at the Pittsfield farm, eager to prove he could carry on the many tasks demanded. At times he may have been the only man on hand for the hard labor. The farm had been his grandfather's originally, and then came into his uncle Thomas's hands. It covered many acres and had a large pond—fun for swimming and skating as the seasons changed. In earlier years, vacationing there, the Melville kids savored its fruits—apples, pears, peaches, cherries. The house itself was "of goodly proportions," Herman wrote later, "with ample hall and staircases, carved woodwork and solid oaken timbers."

From a rock on high ground, Herman had a fine view of the land stretching toward Pittsfield's homes and steeples. He had always enjoyed it on short visits, and as he cultivated the land his affection for it grew stronger and deeper. "For once in his life," biographer Hershel Parker notes, Herman Melville "was where he wanted to be when he wanted to be there."

Late in the summer a cousin, Robert Melvill, two years older, showed up at the farm. He was teaching in the neighborhood, and his experience apparently inspired Herman to become a schoolteacher. We have no record of how he could leave the farm, and who then took it over. But he did find a job in the Pike District School, about 5 miles (8 kilometers) from Pittsfield. He boarded in the house of an old Yankee with twelve children, five of them to be among the thirty pupils he taught. The "schollars," he wrote, were of "all ages, sizes, rank, character and education." Let's hope they learned to spell better than their teacher, for Herman, in the drafts of his books still to come, got a great many words wrong: "Charactor," "hystery," "difficultys," "gennerally," and "intimatly" are a few examples.

On a visit home in January 1838, Herman found his mother about to be evicted from her house for failure to pay rent. She couldn't rely on Herman or Gansevoort to help her make ends meet. She managed to stave off eviction until she found a cheaper house to rent in Lansingburgh, a town of about 500 families, a dozen miles north of Albany, on the eastern side of the Hudson. It was a commercial center for both Hudson River and oceangoing trade.

Giving up teaching after a year, Herman began a surveying and engineering course at the Lansingburgh Academy,

Although it was a step downward in accommodations for the family, Herman Melville's Lansingburgh, New York, home is a literary landmark to this day. It now houses the Lansingburgh Historical Society.

near his mother's home. The tuition was $5.25 for the term. He hoped that at last he had taken the right path to a stable profession.

His uncle, Peter Gansevoort, tried to help by introducing Herman to William C. Bouck, a middle-aged man now one of the five commissioners managing the Erie Canal. Built between 1817 and 1825, the canal extended from Albany to Buffalo and linked the Hudson River with Lake Erie. It had quickly become the chief route for emigrants from New England to the Great Lakes country. Its opening created an agricultural boom in the West. Its success set off a canal-building frenzy. Businessmen lobbied politicians in state and federal legislatures for funding to add waterway links that would improve transportation and thereby speed progress and profits.

Uncle Peter's introductory letter to Bouck praised Herman as "a young man of talent" and said that any job on the canal, "however humble it may be," would be welcome, for his nephew would prefer to start near the bottom "and advance by his own merit."

When nothing came of the application, Herman and his mother knew the family would be even worse off for lack of any money from him. He filled his time by reading books, pamphlets, and newspapers that Gansevoort, now home too, and ailing, had collected. Herman liked especially the novels of Sir Walter Scott and Washington Irving. But over the winter he also read the poetry of Byron and Shakespeare, Milton, and Coleridge.

He read widely too in the accounts of men who had traveled to remote parts of the world—such as Captain James Cook, the English explorer who had sailed into the South Pacific in the 1770s, and Mungo Park, the Scottish explorer who had published his *Travels in the Interior Districts of Africa* in 1799. Park's report revealed to Herman aspects of African humanity very different from the conceptions of Africans held by most Americans at that time. What Park described of their work skills surely surprised him, for the knowledge that Africans brought skills into slavery clashed with the belief of many whites that Africans "were by nature ignorant, hopelessly inferior to whites," as the historian Sterling Stuckey put it.

As a teenager, Herman was learning from these travel accounts about the economic value of slavery to America. (Soon his own experience at work would extend and enrich his understanding.)

With no classes to attend, Herman tried his hand at writing. When a local paper appealed for beginners to send in samples of their writing, he provided some pieces he called "Fragments from a Writing Desk." Two appeared, in May 1839, without his name. The first showed a healthy interest in girls and a flossy prose style, garnished with passages from the great poets of England. In the second he told a romantic story that ended in complete disillusion.

No doubt cheered momentarily by Herman's appearance in print, his mother was soon frantic again when her rent came due. She begged $50 each from her two brothers, expressing the hope that her sons would one day be able to support her. Herman was only able to find work now and then as a hired hand. Gansevoort, after fifteen months at home recovering slowly from his sickness, returned to New York and what he hoped would be a law practice.

What could Herman do? What prospect for a more secure life was open to him? At nineteen, he had only a skimpy, fragmented education to prepare him for business or a profession. But there was one thing a young man in his situation could do. And that was to go to sea.

He had personal examples to follow. Four of his cousins had done just that. And were still doing it. Thomas Melvill had entered the navy as a midshipman in 1830, got into trouble for drinking, and began shipping out on whalers. Three sons of his aunt Mary Gansevoort had also gone to sea while they were boys.

To become a seaman on a whaler or a merchant ship was no way to gain prosperity or prestige. Nor would such a move help his mother financially. A merchant ship? At least it would get him to see some part of Europe. A whaler? The Pacific. In June 1839, Herman took the boat from Albany to New York. There his brother Gansevoort promised to help get him aboard a ship—whaler or merchant.

CHAPTER 4

Merchant Seaman

On June 5, 1839, Herman Melville sailed out of New York Harbor on the *St. Lawrence,* a merchant ship bound for Liverpool, England. It was a small ship, only about 120 feet (36 meters) long and 25 feet (8 meters) wide. Besides cargo—mainly bales of cotton—it carried cabin and steerage passengers.

The *St. Lawrence* took Herman on as cabin boy, for a few dollars a month. The crew list specified that the new man was nineteen, 5' 8/12", of light complexion, with brown hair. From captain on down to cabin boy the crew numbered sixteen, most of them in their twenties and several, like Herman, New Yorkers.

Herman was put to work at once, finding a lot of physical labor was demanded of him—washing down decks, cleaning out chicken coops and pigpens, tidying cabins, helping cook and steward (both of them black men). It was not all strange to him for he had heard many stories of life at sea from his cousins.

This first voyage provided the basis for Melville's autobiographical novel, *Redburn,* which he wrote ten years later. Through his main character, a young sailor named Redburn, Melville re-created shipboard life and Liverpool, his first foreign city. Liverpool was the biggest port in the world at that time. It had been the chief home port for the British slave trade. In one eleven-year period (1783–1793), Liverpool slave ships alone brought over 300,000 slaves to the Americas. By

1800 the city was sending 120 ships a year to the African coast. The whole city, said a Liverpool minister, "was built up by the blood of the poor Africans." Tailors, grocers, tallow-chandlers (candle makers), attorneys—all had shares in fitting the slave ships. The trade used the labor of thousands of boat-builders, carpenters, coopers, riggers, sail makers, glaziers (glass setters), joiners, ironmongers, gunsmiths, and carters. The average net profit for each voyage was 30 percent, and profits of 100 percent were not uncommon.

At the foot of a statue of the naval hero Lord Nelson, Redburn saw "four naked figures in chains, seated in various attitudes of humiliation and despair. . . . Those woebegone fig-ures of captives . . . involuntarily reminded me of four African slaves in the marketplace. . . . And my thoughts would revert to Virginia and Carolina, and also to the historical fact that the African slave-trade once constituted the principal com-merce of Liverpool."

The cotton cargo carried by Herman's ship was raised by slaves in the southern states, and was sold mainly to British textile manufacturers.

In port, the seamen still had many chores aboard ship. They worked from daylight to 4 P.M., when they could go ashore and not return until next morning at daylight. Liverpool was a city Herman's father had known, welcomed into the comfortable homes of the merchants he came to do business with. For seamen it was quite a different Liverpool.

In the novel, Redburn describes the Liverpool that Melville must have seen: "Of all seaports in the world, Liverpool perhaps most abounds in all the variety of land-sharks, land-rats, and the vermin which make the hapless mariner their prey. In the shape of landlords, bar-keepers, clothiers, crimps [members of press-gangs] and boarding-house loungers, the land-sharks devour him limb by limb, while the land-rats and mice constantly nibble at his purse."

While exploring Liverpool, Redburn saw all around him "poverty, poverty, poverty in almost endless vistas." Yet he couldn't help observing that in American cities the poor were mostly black. Yet the victims of poverty in Liverpool were all white. This seems to have surprised Melville as it did his character Redburn who had taken it for granted that poverty is a fate that befalls only blacks. It shocks him to find that poverty knows no color line.

In Liverpool, Redburn notices that the black man "steps with a prouder pace, and lifts his head like a man; for here, no such exaggerated feeling exists in respect to him, as in America." He finds racial prejudice so lacking that when his ship's black steward "walks arm-in-arm with a good-looking English woman" the British take no notice of it. Whereas in New York, Redburn says, "such a couple would have been mobbed within three minutes." He begins to think about prejudice, and how it damages most people, and how hard it is to escape it. But a little reflection showed that, "after all, it was but recognizing his [the black's] claim to humanity and normal equality; so that, in some things, we Americans leave to other countries the carrying out of the principle that stands at the head of our Declaration of Independence."

In his wanderings, Redburn came across street preachers, standing on the steps of public buildings or at the corner of a wharf, wherever they could attract an audience. "I always made a point of joining," he wrote, "and would find myself surrounded by a motley crowd of seamen from all quarters of the globe, and women, and lumpers [longshoremen], and dock laborers of all sorts."

At one such meeting in St. George's Square, Redburn finds "addressing the orderly throng a pale, hollow-eyed young man, who looked worn with much watching, or much toil, or too little food. . . . In his hand was a soiled inflammatory looking pamphlet from which he frequently read. . . . I was not long

*A*lthough the port of Liverpool was reminiscent of his native New York, Melville found the social mores very different. He was particularly struck by the absence of racial prejudice.

within hearing of him before I became aware that this youth was a Chartist. I do not know why, but I thought he must be some despairing elder son, supporting by hard toil his mother and sisters, for of such many political desperadoes are made."

The Chartists were a year-old movement of workmen demanding that Parliament enact universal suffrage for men, whether property owners or not. Their platform was embodied in a document called the People's Charter. Back home in America similar movements were springing up to extend democratic rights and economic opportunity for all.

Many merchant ships did not sail on a fixed schedule, but only when the shipowner's quota for cargo and passengers was filled. The *St. Lawrence,* ready at last, cleared Liverpool on August 14, two weeks after Herman turned twenty.

By this time, transatlantic ships had increased their speed and improved their accommodations, so that first-class passengers could enjoy the comforts of hotel living. But conditions for steerage passengers were miserable. Emigrants fleeing poverty or persecution in their homelands were desperate to reach a better life in America. And shippers packed them in like cattle.

Although the potato famine would not devastate Ireland for another several years, there were many Irish leaving home for America to seek a better life and freedom from British rule. And others too—Germans, Scandinavians, people from all parts of Europe. Melville joined the crew in preparing rough quarters for the emigrants in steerage. Four rows of bunks, three tiers one above another, were rapidly knocked together with coarse planks. "They looked more like dog kennels than anything else; especially as the place was so gloomy and dark, no light coming down except through the fore and after hatchways." The galley for the steerage passengers "was a large open

The crowded decks of this ship leaving Liverpool for America hints at what conditions must have been like with all onboard huddled belowdecks in stormy weather.

stove, or iron range—made expressly for emigrant ships, wholly unprotected from the weather, and where alone the emigrants are permitted to cook their food while at sea." Every meal was oatmeal and water, boiled into what they called "mush."

There were storms at sea on the homeward passage and the agonized vomiting in steerage was so extreme, he said, that "to hold your head down the fore hatchway was like holding it down a suddenly exposed cesspool."

The voyage took about seven weeks. On September 30, 1839, the *St. Lawrence* docked at a wharf off South Street in Manhattan. At sunrise the next day, the crew was released. Melville's first voyage—a time for learning and growth—was over. Once again, he had to decide what to do next.

CHAPTER 5

Dwarfs, Not Titans

Herman's first move was to visit his mother in Lansingburgh. With no sign of economic recovery visible, Mrs. Melville's worries were worse than ever. One creditor was even threatening to take away all her furniture. Peter Gansevoort, on whose aid she had relied in the past, was himself hit hard by the economic depression.

Herman scoured the neighboring towns for work and found a teaching job at the Greenbush and Schodack Academy across the Hudson from Albany. This time he had spruced himself up before he applied for the post. The family had long deplored his indifference to personal appearance. He would wear any old rag, fail to shave, and let his hair grow long and wild. That wouldn't do for a teacher. He boarded with a local family and late on Friday afternoons crossed the river and then walked 15 miles (24 kilometers), much of it in the dark, to spend the weekend with his family.

That fall an ancient conflict in the district between tenant farmers and landlords erupted in near-civil war. It was a case of poor common folk against exploiting aristocrats. And the aristocrats were Herman's blood relatives, the Van Rensselaers. Back in the time of Dutch rule, that family had been given perpetual leases on huge tracts of land with their tenants obliged to pay annual rent in services, crops, and money. But the soil had been exhausted and the poor farmers had organized to put an end to the feudal system of perpetual obligation. When the Van Rensselaer family attempted to collect $400,000 in back rents, the Anti-Rent War broke out. Hundreds of farmers, mounted on horses, blocked the roads as the sheriff's posse advanced on their land to force payment or make arrests. Not until 1846 did progressive changes in state law end the troubles.

Herman was proud of his Dutch heritage, but the family ties had done nothing to bring prosperity or happiness to his parents or their children. Nor had the Van Rensselaer cousins invited any personal intimacy. What Herman's inner feeling must have been comes out in the way he portrays the young Redburn in his novel. "There is no misanthrope like a boy disappointed," Redburn says, a boy with "that desperation and recklessness of poverty which only a pauper knows." And Redburn thinks back to the time "when his father became bankrupt, and died," and "his mother was no longer bright and happy."

All the more bitter for Redburn "was to think of how well off were my cousins, who were happy and rich, and lived at home with my uncles and aunts, with no thought of going to sea for a living."

Soon after *Redburn* appeared in 1849, however, some of the Van Rensselaers would become friendlier with the Melville family.

It was about this time that Herman became increasingly aware of public discussion over literary failure. Many Europeans and even some Americans had begun to claim that while the young nation had made a great contribution to the advancement of democracy, it was a miserable disappointment in cultural matters. A British wit asked, "In the four quarters of the globe, who reads an American book? or goes to an American play? or looks at an American picture or statue?" The answer was, "Nobody." Frances Trollope, an Englishwoman traveling in America, described American art and literature as "trash" and a "mass of slip-slop."

Governor Seward called the militia into play, thus creating the Anti-Rent "War," when a confrontation between farmers and a sheriff's posse got out of control.

One of the most brilliant foreigners to inspect America was the French writer and politician Alexis de Tocqueville. He reported that "in few of the civilized nations of our time have the higher sciences made less progress than in the United States, and in few have great artists, distinguished poets, or celebrated writers been more rare."

Even the Concord sage Ralph Waldo Emerson, in 1838 pointed out that his country had not fulfilled the great expectations of mankind following our great revolution. Dwarfs, not

Titans, were the only figures visible in the world of the arts.

In November 1839 a Troy newspaper that Herman read reprinted a magazine article that said in part:

> And our literature! Oh, when will it breathe the spirit of our republican institutions? When will it be imbued with the God-like aspiration of intellectual freedom—the elevating principle of equality? When will it assert its national independence, and speak the soul—the heart of the American people? Why do our authors aim at no higher degree of merit, than a successful imitation of English writers of celebrity?

Still only twenty, Herman had not yet ventured into poetry or fiction. His eloquence funneled into debate, not onto paper. But laments over the failure of American writers to rise to great heights may have set him thinking: What might I do one day?

Meanwhile his mother, pushing pride aside, wrote to her two brothers saying "it isn't possible that you've left me to struggle with absolute want. When I pay off every cent you send me to those I owe, in a few days I'm poor again. I can hear you say the times are hard, tis true—if I could postpone my wants until the times become easy, I would do it with all my heart."

With five children (four daughters and a ten-year-old son) still living at home, she estimated her expense to run to $50 a month. Rent, food, fuel—they consumed most of it with little or nothing left for clothing. Despite her distress, she felt "cheered by Herman's prospects. . . . He appears to be interested in his occupation—he has a great charge, and deep responsibility is attached to the education of 60 scholars."

To care for sixty students was a great burden. Herman, always back home on weekends, probably had no time to make friends with fellow teachers. After he became famous, none of his students or colleagues are known to have published any impressions of him.

Herman's brother Gansevoort wrote him from New York and sent him newspapers too, but Herman rarely replied. This the older brother blamed on Herman's habit of always putting things off till later—and then not doing them.

Month after month passed at Herman's school, yet he was never paid. It meant that he could not pay his rent at the boardinghouse. The school too was a victim of the depression. Herman wondered if he'd ever land a job that would actually pay him enough for a decent living.

He talked it over with his old school chum, Eli Fly. Although Eli had a decent job, he agreed that life in the western lands might be more promising. They made plans to go west, to the young state of Illinois, where Herman's Uncle Thomas and Aunt Mary were thought to be doing well on the farm in Galena.

That spring the Greenbush and Schodack Academy shut down for lack of funds. No teachers were paid for the work they'd put in. Herman at once scouted for work, taking short-term jobs when he could find them. At one point he filled in as teacher in Brunswick, just northeast of Troy, but the school failed to pay him the $6 promised. That clinched it. He and Eli would join thousands of other unemployed young men heading west to seek their fortunes. Eli was an experienced law clerk and Herman could both teach and do surveying.

What the two didn't know was that business in Illinois was "in a most lamentable condition." Ignorant but hopeful, early in June 1840, Herman and Eli boarded a boat on the Erie Canal for the three-day trip from Albany to Buffalo. Then by other means to Toledo, Detroit, Milwaukee, Chicago, and finally Galena, across the prairie from Lake Michigan. By now it was early July.

As soon as they arrived they found that Uncle Thomas was in no condition to help them. Now sixty-four, and sick, he no longer owned the farm. In fact he had been working in a

The 1830s

The decade of the 1830s saw great changes in American life. When it started, the population of the United States was nearly 13 million, including 2.3 million African Americans. The great majority of people lived in rural regions or small towns. Steam locomotives were beginning to haul passengers and freight faster and farther and cheaper than the old horse-and-wagon or stagecoach. The Native Americans were being forced by congressional law, despite bloody resistance, from their ancestral lands in the Southeast to territory west of the Mississippi. Cotton cultivated by slaves was king, supporting the planter economy of the South and enabling southern legislators, executives, and federal judges to exert their influence on the public life of the country.

A movement to abolish slavery was getting under way, with abolitionist newspapers and the American Anti-Slavery Society spreading the message. The grain reaper, sewing machine, and telegraph were among the American inventions improving production and communication. In Ohio, Oberlin College was established, the first to admit both men and women, and blacks. The first baseball diamond was laid out in Cooperstown, New York, and the first teachers college opened in Lexington, Massachusetts.

In what would soon be Melville's field, the public was reading James Fenimore Cooper, Edgar Allan Poe, John Greenleaf Whittier, Ralph Waldo Emerson, Washington Irving, Nathaniel Hawthorne, Henry Wadsworth Longfellow, and William Cullen Bryant. These are some of the significant facts and developments that provide the broad background of the young Melville's life.

store, managing it until the owner accused him of stealing from the till. It was an old pattern for Uncle Thomas. Back in Massachusetts, he had been jailed more than once for not paying debts, and even accused of fraud. It was a painful ending to Herman's illusions about his uncle. As a young man, hadn't Thomas Melvill Jr. traveled in Europe during the Napoleonic Wars, seen the emperor with his own eyes, dined with Lafayette, talked with Thomas Jefferson? True, all true, but nothing had ever come of that promising beginning. Five years later, Uncle Thomas would die in Galena.

Herman and Eli turned back almost at once. They were home again around August 1. It had been a fruitless venture, except for the fresh sights they saw on their travels. But lovely landscapes don't put pennies in the pocket.

CHAPTER 6

---✦✕✦---

Chasing Whales

When Herman showed up again in New York, big brother got him into a cheap boardinghouse: $2.50 a week, but no dinners. It was near the Hudson, and he began to hunt for work. He had arrived in shaggy hair and thick beard, and Gansevoort would have none of that. You can't apply for a job looking like a tramp! So Herman had his hair sheared and his beard shaved. "Now you look more like a Christian than usual," Gansevoort said.

Since Herman had left home nearly broke, and returned completely broke, his brother took him to dinner every night, observing that Herman still had the voracious—and costly— appetite of a growing boy. Friend Eli Fly had a fine handwriting and found a job quickly, sitting at a desk copying documents all day long. Herman's hand was atrocious, however. (Later his manuscripts would have to be heroically copied for editors by his wife or his sisters. They would try to correct his misspellings too.)

While making the rounds for a job, Herman was reading a new book, *Two Years Before the Mast*, by Richard Henry Dana Jr. Dana had taken off time from his studies at Harvard and spent two years at sea (1834–1836) as a common sailor. (After this, he returned to Harvard for his degree.) The new book was an absorbing account of Dana's voyage. It described rounding Cape Horn, storms at sea, and the little-known California territory, then still part of Mexico.

Upon his return to New York, the dockside ambience left a lasting impression on Melville. Detailed descriptions of harbor scenes appear again and again in his works.

But Dana also reported the abuses he and his mates suffered aboard ship. Wrongs he was determined to set right. After earning a law degree, he battled for seamen's rights and for the abolition of slavery.

Herman read Dana's book intently, comparing it with his own experience at sea. Years later he wrote Dana that reading his book had made him feel "tied and welded to you by a sort of Siamese link of affectionate sympathy."

It was around this time too that Herman read a sensational piece in the *Knickerbocker* magazine about the capture in the Pacific of a great white sperm whale called Mocha Dick.

It's likely that reading these accounts led Herman to go to sea again, but this time on a whaler.

It was, in fact, not an unusual choice to make. Hadn't several cousins already done it? As one historian put it, "America was born of the sea and spent a great part of its youthful energies on deep water." Many settlers clung to the ocean's edge for food and for a living. With so many villages and towns along the coast, few youngsters could escape the thought of a sailor's life. Timber was everywhere and skilled craftsmen worked it into ships—for the merchant marine, the navy, and the whalers.

The New York waterfront, Herman writes, was lined with "thousands and thousands of mortal men fixed in ocean reveries. Some leaning against the spiles [posts]; some seated upon the pier-heads; some looking over the bulwarks of ships from China; some high aloft in the rigging, as if striving to get a still better seaward peep. But all these landsmen, of weekdays pent up in lath and plaster, tied to counters, nailed to benches, clinched to desks. . . . They must get just as nigh the water as they possibly can without falling in. . . ."

It was not a new trade that Herman was trying to enter, but a time-honored one. For generations, whalemen from New Bedford and Nantucket had been chasing their game around Cape Horn into what Melville called "the remotest secret drawers and lockers of the world." And now, as he was about to join the trade, "American whalers had practically staked out the broad Pacific as their own green pasture."

Whaling was one of the leading industries of Massachusetts, bringing in millions of dollars every year. But, as Herman knew from his cousins, whaling was no pleasure cruise. It was an infernal and stinking business, a small-scale hell for whalemen.

The owners of whaleships recruited seamen at shipping offices in New York and Boston. Herman saw one of their "WHALEMEN WANTED" posters and with Gansevoort set out for New Bedford to apply. Not that big brother meant to go to sea;

he was still concerned to get young Herman started right. There Herman found a new ship, the *Acushnet*, and signed on as "Green Hand," with his share set at 1/175th of the profits of the voyage. After all expenses were paid, the profits of a voyage would be divided up among the owners and crew, each one getting a traditional part called a lay.

The ship, with two decks and three masts, was about 105 feet (32 meters) long and 28 feet (8 meters) wide, and weighed 359 tons. As he signed on, Herman was advanced $84 "on the strength of future services and earnings."

And then the brothers parted. Before returning to New York, Gansevoort decided to visit his aunts in Boston and to call on his father's old friend, Lemuel Shaw. A lawyer long active in state politics, Shaw, now about sixty, had been chief justice of the Massachusetts Supreme Court for the past ten years. He was an old friend of the Melvill family, and especially of Allan Melvill, Herman's father. (One of Judge Shaw's children, Elizabeth, would one day become Herman's wife.)

The captain of Herman's ship was Valentine Pease, a Nantucketer of forty-three, on his last voyage. He and the mates slept aft, with the skilled men (boat steerers, carpenter, cook, steward, and cooper) bunking nearby. The other twenty men lived in the forecastle, a little room where they stored chests, clothing, and bedding for what might be a cruise of three or more years. They slept in bunks ranged along the wall and across the bulkhead, ten bunks in all, two men to a bunk.

Most of the crew were in their twenties, a few in their teens, and the rest, the more skilled, in their thirties. Many of them would desert ship during the long voyage, with the captain having to replace the missing with men recruited at whatever ports they stopped at.

The ship's cook was black, as were two other seamen. African Americans were not unknown on the sea. One esti-

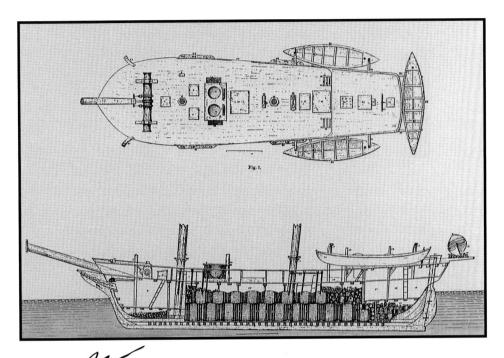

Fig. 1.

Whaling ships of Melville's day were rugged and dependable, built to stand the crushing ice of the Arctic and the typhoons of the South Seas. The hold was divided into upper and lower decks and mainly used to carry casks.

mate holds that at least one sailor in six was black. In this field of labor, the scholar Louis Filler says, "workingmen met the Negro with a degree of camaraderie, if not cooperation. Brutalized, despised, toiling under conditions which differed only in details from that of the slave, with no status on shipboard and little before the law, the northern seaman had no logical reason to esteem himself the Negro's superior."

On January 3, 1841, Herman's ship sailed out of the cold winter weather, south to the Bahamas, where the *Acushnet* found its first whales. They reaped enough to come into Rio de Janeiro with 150 barrels of sperm oil. The average whale, about 19 tons, was 40 feet (12 meters) long, and yielded around 25 to 40 barrels of oil. The experts at the Mystic

Seaport in Connecticut say it often took about three days to "cut in" (slice off the skin) and "try out" (boil the skin to get oil from the blubber) a single bowhead whale. But the much larger sperm whale required four days of work.

What was it like to chase after a whale? Melville himself, years after his *Acushnet* voyage and before he wrote *Moby-Dick*, tells us in his review of a book about whaling by J. Ross Browne:

> My young friends, just fancy yourselves, for the first time in an open boat (so slight that three men might walk off with it), some 12 or 15 miles from your ship & about a hundred times as far from the nearest land, giving chase to one of the oleaginous monsters. "Pull, Pull, you lubberly nay-makers!" cries the boat-header jumping up & down in the stern-sheets in a frenzy of professional excitement, while the gasping admirers of Captain Marryatt & the sea, tug with might & main at the buckling oars—"Pull, Pull, I say; Break your lazy backs!" Presently the whale is within "darting distance" & you hear the roar of the waters in his wake.—How palpitating the hearts of the frightened oarsmen at this interesting juncture! My young friends, just turn round & snatch a look at that whale—. There he goes, surging through the brine, which ripples about his vast head as if it were the bow of a ship. Believe me, it's quite as terrible as going into battle to a raw recruit.
>
> "Stand up & give it to him!" shrieks the boat-header at the steering-oar to the harpooneer in the bow. The latter drops his oar & snatches his "iron." It flies from his hands—& where are we then, my lovelies?—It's all a mist, a crash,—a horrible blending of sounds & sights, as the agonized whale lashes the water around him into suds and vapor—dashes the boat aside, & at last rushes, madly, thro' the water towing after him the half-filled craft which rocks from side to side while the disordered crew clutch at the

Melville was able to describe for his readers the sensations that a whaler might experience aboard a small boat chasing a creature hundreds of times larger than a man.

gunwhale to avoid being tossed out. Meanwhile all sorts of horrific edged tools—lances, harpoons & spades—are slipping about; and the imminent line itself—smoking round the logger-head and passing along the entire length of the boat—is almost death to handle, tho' it grazes your person.

But all this is nothing to what follows. As yet, you have but simply fastened to the whale; he must be fought & killed.

The folks at home got news of their loved ones awhaling only sporadically. Seaport newspapers ran reports of ship sightings as homeward-bound vessels relayed the news. Letters Melville wrote home might pass from ship to ship as they met on the ocean or in ports. In the same way, barrels of oil collected by one whaler would be passed to another, bound for home and with room for the added cargo.

Nantucket!

By Melville's time, many towns on the coasts of New England and Long Island—even along the Hudson—had their whaling fleets. The first port had been Nantucket, a sand island in the Atlantic, south of Cape Cod. On its barren soil you could raise no crops; so the island's life was linked with seafaring and whaling. The island's Quaker people became famous as among the best and most daring seamen in the world.

Here is Melville's lyrical description of the island, from *Moby-Dick*:

Nantucket! Take out your map and look at it. See what a real corner of the world it occupies; how it stands there, away off shore, more lonely than the Eddystone lighthouse. Look at it—a mere hillock, an elbow of sand; all beach, without a background. There is more sand there than you would use in twenty years as a substitute for blotting paper. Some gamesome wights [wits] will tell you that they have to plant weeds there, they don't grow naturally; that they import Canada thistles; that they have to send beyond seas for a spile to stop a leak in an oil cask; that pieces of wood in Nantucket are carried about like bits of the true cross in Rome; that people there plant toadstools before their houses, to get under the shade in summer time; that one blade of grass makes an oasis, three blades in a day's walk a prairie; that they wear quicksand shoes, something like Laplander snowshoes; that they are so shut up, belted about, every way inclosed, surrounded, and made an utter island of by the ocean, that to their very chairs and tables small clams will sometimes be found adhering, as to the backs of sea turtles. . . .

What wonder, then, that these Nantucketers, born on a beach, should take to the sea for a livelihood! They first caught crabs and quohogs in the sand; grown bolder, they waded out

Melville described Nantucket Island as "…a mere hillock, an elbow of sand; all beach, without a background."

with nets for mackerel; more experienced, they pushed off in boats and captured cod; and at last, launching a navy of great ships on the sea, explored this watery world; put an incessant belt of circumnavigations round it; peeped in at Bhering's Straits; and in all seasons and all oceans declared everlasting war with the mightiest animated mass that has survived the flood; most monstrous and most mountainous! That Himmalehan, salt-sea Mastodon, clothed with such portentousness of unconscious power, that his very panics are more to be dreaded than his most fearless and malicious assaults!

The prime target of the man of Nantucket was the leviathan of whales, the sperm whale. Until the Civil War the sperm was America's main source of artificial light, and the only smokeless and odorless fuel available. Sperm candles were made of the oil found by the hundred gallons in the whale's head. And great quantities of oil were extracted from the whale's blubber, the casing of fat around the body. The market for it was huge, for the oil lighted lamps, public buildings, and city streets; it lubricated machinery, and processed leather. Almost as valuable was whalebone, or baleen, long thin bones with great elasticity, ideal for ladies' corsets.

In April the *Acushnet* sailed around Cape Horn and up the coast of Chile. In the next few weeks they sighted sperm whales but were not able to take any. Writing home, Melville said his crew had better morale than most whalers could expect, but that was probably meant to make the family feel good.

In the Pacific cruising waters, Herman and his mates visited with sister ships bent on the same mission. Sometimes they hunted in packs for their prey. With seamen from all around the world, there were stories aplenty to be told in the forecastle during the long days and nights. Without a good story or a good song, the men would have perished of the monotony. During the dogwatch at night and the watch below, a song was always popular, accompanied by a harmonica, a fiddle, a concertina, a pipe, or a pennywhistle. On deck, as the sailors heaved on the capstan or at the line, they couldn't do without their work songs, called shanties.

CHAPTER 7

Tropical Paradise

Night watch on deck: the best time for swapping stories with shipmates. As the *Acushnet* sailed close to the equator, Herman heard about the terrible tragedy of an old whaleship, the *Essex*. The disaster had occurred twenty years before, but whalemen could not stop telling and retelling the tale.

The story was wondrous and terrifying. On November 20, 1820, a huge sperm whale had rammed headlong into the *Essex* as the ship was sailing in the Pacific, far west of the Galápagos Islands. The *Essex* began to founder, as if she had struck a great rock. With the panicky crew rushing to abandon ship, the whale veered round, and at twice its usual speed, again rammed the sinking *Essex*, punching a great hole in her bow.

What followed was a horrifying tale of murder and cannibalism. The survivors were a thousand miles from the nearest land. They managed somehow to carry supplies of bread and water off the foundering *Essex* to stow in the three small whaleboats.

When they had rowed only a few boat lengths away, the *Essex* capsized behind them. A cry of horror and despair burst from every man as their ship vanished below the water. What had possessed the great beast? Were the *Essex* and her crew the victims of a whale's malignant mischief? Could it have been God's design that their ship should go down?

This etching from The Mariner's Chronicle *is entitled "The Essex Struck by a Whale!" The whale is nearly as long as the entire ship.*

As days and weeks on the open sea went by, the three boats tried, but failed, to stay together. Losing sight of one another, their hope of rescue began to fade.

Of the twenty men who escaped the sinking ship, only eight would survive. One whaleboat disappeared; no one ever knew what happened to it. The men in another boat were rescued by a Nantucket whaler.

Then, on the morning of February 23, 1821—sixty-four days after the whale had sunk the *Essex*—another ship out of Nantucket spied a small boat floating aimlessly in the sea. Moving up, the sailors looked down into the boat. They saw two men curled up at opposite ends, gnawing madly on a few bones of the many scattered around them.

It turned out that when their bread and water were gone, and hunger and thirst had reduced them to near skeletons, the whalemen from the *Essex* had decided upon the only way at least some might survive. They drew lots to determine which man would be killed, and then lots to determine who would kill him.

One man was killed, and then eaten. And as no rescue ship came in sight, another, and another, and another . . . until only these two delirious ones were left.

Ten years later, building in part upon the account of Owen Chase, first mate on the *Essex*, Melville would write his novel *Moby-Dick*. Although Chase's narrative was published in 1821, Herman had not read it before the tale took root in his imagination as the *Acushnet* sailed through the same waters as the *Essex*.

Late in October the *Acushnet* crossed the equator heading north. The crew soon sighted the Galápagos Islands. (It was on these islands that English naturalist Charles Darwin during his voyage on the *Beagle* made the observations that would lead to his theory of evolution by natural selection.) Melville himself, in 1854, would write several short sketches about them, called "The Encantadas, Enchanted Islands."

In the sketches, he gives his impression of the Galápagos:

> Take five-and-twenty heaps of cinders dumped here and
> there in an outside city lot; imagine some of them magnified
> into mountains, and the vacant lot the sea; and you will

have a fit idea of the general aspect of the Encantadas, or
Enchanted Isles. A group rather of extinct volcanoes than
of isles; looking much as the world at large might, after a
penal conflagration. . . .

But the special curse, as one may call it, of the
Encantadas, that which exalts them in desolation above
Idumea and the Pole, is that to them change never comes;
neither the change of seasons nor of sorrows. Cut by the
Equator, they know no autumn and they know not spring;
while already reduced to the lees of fire, ruin itself can work
little more upon them. The showers refresh the deserts, but
in these isles, rain never falls.

In November the *Acushnet* spotted sperm whales, and probably made a killing before approaching the coast of Peru,
where it anchored at Tombez. By now Herman had been at
sea a long time. What he experienced day by day is not doc-
umented. He kept no diary or log. We know of it only from
the books he wrote later, and these of course were fictional.
Yet it's apparent that he found whaling to be even harsher
than he expected. His cousins' stories did not fully prepare
him for the reality.

This had two aspects: on one side, the thrill; on the other,
the despair. Take the thrilling chase, when the lookout high in
the crow's nest, cries, "There she blows!" Melville describes it
in *Moby-Dick:*

It was a sight full of quick wonder and awe! The vast swells
of the omnipotent sea; the singing, hollow roar they made,
as they rolled along the eight gunwales, like gigantic bowls
in a boundless bowling green; the brief suspended agony of
the boat, as it would tip for an instant on the knifelike edge
of the sharper waves that almost seemed threatening to cut
it in two; the sudden profound dip into the watery glens and
hollows; the keen spurrings and goadings to gain the top of
the opposite hill; the headlong, sledlike slide down its other

side—all these, with the cries of the headsmen and har-
pooners, and the shuddering gasps of the oarsmen, with the
wondrous sight of the ivory *Pequod* bearing down upon her
boats with outstretched sails, like a wild hen after her
screaming brood; all this was thrilling. Not the raw recruit,
marching from the bosom of his wife into the fever heat of
his first battle; not the dead man's ghost encountering the
first unknown phantom in the other world—neither of
these can feel stranger and stronger emotions than that man
does, who for the first time finds himself putting into the
charmed, churned circle of the hunted sperm whale . . . A
short rushing sound leaped out of the boat, it was the darted
iron of Queequeg. Then all in one welded commotion came
an invisible push from astern, while forward the boat
seemed striking on a ledge; the sail collapsed and exploded;
a gush of scalding vapor shot up near by; something rolled
and tumbled like an earthquake beneath us. The whole
crew were half suffocated as they were tossed helter-skelter
into the white curdling cream of the squall. Squall, whale,
and harpoon had all blended together. . . .

And the despair: Not many men chose to repeat a whaling
cruise. Reported J. Ross Browne of his own experiences:

> There is a murderous appearance about the blood-stained
> decks, and the huge masses of flesh and blubber lying here
> and there. . . . The forecastle was black and slimy with filth;
> very small, and as hot as an oven. It was filled with a com-
> pound of foul air, smoke, sea-chests, soap-kegs, greasy pans,
> tainted meat, Portuguese ruffians, and sea-sick Americans. . . .
> From the time he leaves port [the whaler] is beyond the
> sphere of human rights, he is a slave until he returns. All
> this time he is subject to . . . such treatment as an ignorant
> and tyrannical master . . . chooses to inflict upon him.

There is no record of Captain Pease abusing the crew. But in
Typee, Melville's first novel, he would describe conditions on

a whaler leading to mutiny, when Tom, the first-person narrator, jumps ship because the captain is "tyrannical" and "inhuman." So bad a leader that mutiny seems inevitable. Yet "unfortunately, with very few exceptions," says Melville's protagonist, "our crew was composed of a parcel of dastardly and mean-spirited wretches, divided among themselves, and only united in enduring without resistance the unmitigated tyranny of the captain."

In the last days of 1841 and the first months of 1842 the *Acushnet* sighted sperm whales but seems to have captured none. By June, however, she had seventy-five barrels aboard, and sent home two hundred on another ship. It was only natural that in these long months away from home, away from women, the men would think it wonderful if they could stay on one of the tropical islands they heard of, where they could taste fresh fruit, eat good meat, and enjoy the company of women.

And then it happened. Captain Pease announces that to take aboard more supplies they are heading for the Marquesas, a group of twelve mountainous islands about 740 miles (1,190 kilometers) northeast of Tahiti in the South Pacific. The crew had not seen land since January. Melville was not the only man aboard never to have seen a Polynesian island. Their goal was Nukahiva, the largest island. The whalemen all had heard stories of ferocious islanders who loved to kill and cook people to satisfy their cannibal appetites. But also stories of lovely island girls.

On June 23, 1842, the *Acushnet* entered the island's bay. The scenery astonishes the men, who have known nothing but empty ocean for months. In *Typee*, Tom says he saw "bold rock-bound coasts, with the surf beating high against the lofty cliffs, and broken here and there into deep inlets, which open to the view thickly wooded valleys, separated by the spurs of mountains clothed with tufted grass, and sweeping down towards the sea from an elevated and furrowed interior."

As they sail in, Tom notices a singular commotion in the water ahead of the vessel:

At first I imagined it to be produced by a shoal of fish sporting on the surface, but it was caused by a shoal of "whinhenies" (young girls), who in this manner were coming off from the shore to welcome us. As they drew nearer, and I watched the rising and sinking of their forms, and beheld the uplifted right arm bearing above the water the girdle of tappa, and their long dark hair trailing beside them as they swam, I almost fancied they could be nothing else than so many mermaids—and very like mermaids they behaved too.

We were still some distance from the beach, and under slow headway, when we sailed right into the midst of these swimming nymphs, and they boarded us at every quarter; many seizing hold of the chainplates and springing into the chains; others, at the peril of being run over by the vessel in her course, catching at the bob-stays, and wreathing their slender forms about the ropes, hung suspended in the air. All of them at length succeeded in getting up the ship's side, where they clung dripping with the brine and glowing from the bath, their jet-black tresses streaming over their shoulders, and half enveloping their otherwise naked forms. There they hung, sparkling with savage vivacity, laughing gaily at one another, and chattering away with infinite glee. Nor were they idle the while, for each one performed the simple offices of the toilet for the other. Their luxuriant locks, wound up and twisted into the smallest possible compass, were freed from the briny element; the whole person carefully dried and, from a little round shell that passed from hand to hand, anointed with a fragrant oil; their adornments were completed by passing a few loose folds of white tappa, in a modest cincture, around the waist.

Thus arrayed they no longer hesitated, but flung themselves lightly over the bulwarks, and were quickly frolicking about the decks. Many of them went forward, perching

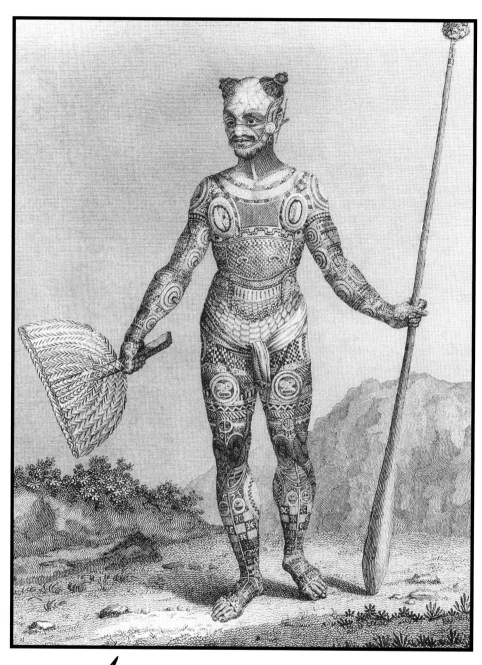

𝒜lthough the women of the island of Nukahiva were
an amazing sight to Melville and his shipmates,
the men were equally as startling to the Western eye.

upon the head-rails or running out upon the bowsprit, while others seated themselves upon the taffrail, or reclined at full length upon the boats. What a sight for us bachelor sailors! How avoid so dire a temptation? For who could think of tumbling these artless creatures overboard, when they had swam miles to welcome us?

Their appearance perfectly amazed me; their extreme youth, the light clear brown of their complexions, their delicate features, and inexpressibly graceful figures, their softly moulded limbs, and free unstudied action, seemed as strange as beautiful. . . .

In the evening after we had come to an anchor the deck was illumined with lanterns, and this picturesque band of sylphs, tricked out with flowers, and dressed in robes of variegated tappa, got up a ball in great style. These females are passionately fond of dancing, and in the wild grace and spirit of their style excel everything that I have ever seen. The varied dances of the Marquesan girls are beautiful in the extreme, but there is an abandoned voluptuousness in their character which I dare not attempt to describe.

Cannibalism

Hearing of what happened to the crew after the whale sank the *Essex* gives one the shivers. Cannibalism—the eating of human flesh by other humans—was practiced in some ancient societies, according to research. It has been noted in Africa, North and South America, the West Indies, and the South Pacific islands where Melville sailed.

The best-known case of it in the Americas is that of the Aztecs, the Indian people of central Mexico at the time of the Spanish conquest, who ate their prisoners of war. Scientific studies hold that the eating of human flesh is almost always a ritual practice.

Rarely does an *Essex* tragedy happen, and only in the most extreme circumstances. Under pressure of prolonged famine, or isolation because of a snowstorm, or an airplane crash, or a shipwreck, people may turn to it in agonized desperation. One of the most famous historical examples occurred in the winter of 1846–1847, when a wagon train of emigrants on the way to California, known now as the Donner party, were trapped by a great snowstorm in the Sierra Nevada mountains. When their limited food gave out, their suffering grew so intense that the surviving members of the expedition were driven to cannibalism.

An earlier instance took place late in 1528. The Spanish conquistador, Cabeza de Vaca, who explored Florida, was wintering with his men on a small island off the coast. Terribly bad weather set in, and without charts or instruments the small groups were stranded. One party began to starve to death, "and the five Christians," de Vaca reported, "came to such straits that they ate one another until only one was left. This one survived only because there was no one left to eat him."

A German explorer made this sketch in the late sixteenth century.
It shows South American Indians carrying a prisoner toward a fire
over which he will be cooked.

CHAPTER 8

From Tahiti to Honolulu

The American whaler was not the only vessel at anchorage in the bay. Three weeks before the *Acushnet* arrived, a huge French warship, *La Reine Blanche*, had sailed in with the admiral announcing that he was taking possession of the Marquesas Islands in the name of France.

It seems the French intended to make a penal colony of the island (as the British had done with Australia), and were building a fort there. So much for the Marquesas remaining a tropical paradise. . . .

But Melville had his mind on other matters. With his closest shipmate, Richard Tobias Greene, called Toby in *Typee*, he was planning to desert the *Acushnet*. After eighteen months aboard they had had enough of whaling. What better place to launch a new life than this lush island? They knew that if caught, they'd be tried for desertion. Nor were they deterred by rumors that stray white men were considered delicious meals for island cannibals.

In *Typee*, Melville (as Tom) admits that in deserting he had broken his contract to serve for the period of the voyage. But he claims that the captain had failed to uphold his side of the contract when he skimped on the food, neglected the sick seamen, and treated the crew like a tyrant.

The *Acushnet* would stay at sea for four and a half years, and in that time half the crew would desert, one would com-

A portrait of Richard T. Greene ("Toby" in Typee*) who deserted ship with Melville at Nukahiva.*

mit suicide, and two would die of venereal disease. On the return voyage, two of the mates would jump ship. Only eleven men were aboard when the whaler reached its home port.

When Melville and Greene got shore leave on July 9, they quietly separated from their shipmates and headed north into the mountains. That night a torrential rain fell. While sheltering under bushes, Herman appears to have been bitten by a venomous reptile, for his leg swelled badly and painfully. While they debated which valley to head for, the *Acushnet* upped anchor and moved out of the bay, giving up on finding the fugitives.

Climbing steep cliffs and working their way through uninhabited wooded valleys the men come across a valley with handsome bamboo buildings. Should they walk in? Were these friendly people? Or a fierce tribe of cannibals?

The Typee tribe proved to be hospitable, even giving Melville nursing care for his infected leg. But the fugitives never meant to make a home here. Their aim was to wait out their ship's departure and then sign on to whatever ship might anchor in the bay.

Greene slipped away, reaching a ship in the harbor. He meant to obtain medicine, and men to carry Melville off the island. But the ship's captain refused to stay, and forced Greene to stay aboard. (The two, Melville and Greene, would not meet again for many years, until after *Typee* was published.)

In the novel, Tom stays on alone, taken care of by an island family. Their son, Kory-Kory, cares for the disabled Tom, carries him about on his back, feeding him, sleeping beside him. As Tom's leg heals, he gradually goes native, finding the Typee way of life warm and peaceful. The family seems determined to keep Tom with them permanently. Their lovely daughter, Fayaway, becomes his intimate companion.

In one chapter of the book, Tom compares his own civilization with the native way of life, and decides theirs is much the better: "There were none of those thousand sources of irritation that the ingenuity of civilized man has created to mar his own felicity." Even the enmity between the Typee and the neighboring Happar people seems mild compared with "civilized" warfare. A skirmish caused only a bruise, a puncture, maybe a missing finger.

Near the end of the book, however, Tom comes across evidence of cannibalism. He finds three packages covered in the native cloth hanging from a pole, and forces his way into a ritual circle where the natives are examining them. The packages contain three preserved human heads, one of them a white man's head. Although the villagers try to convince Tom that all three heads were taken from Happar warriors killed in combat, he can't believe it. Terrified, he wonders how he can flee before they kill and eat him.

A week later, the men of Happar invade the Typees. And to Tom's horror, it ends in a feast with the bodies of the slain Happars.

*A*n illustration from an early version of Typee shows the
beautiful Fayaway with Tom at her feet.

In the end, Tom manages to escape, and finds passage on a whaleship. Although Melville stayed only four weeks on the island, in the novel he stretches it out to four months. He wanted room to re-create a native life in detail and to offer his thoughts on what it signified. He freely criticized the merchant ships and missionaries he believed were infesting the islands:

> The enormities perpetrated in the South Seas upon some inoffensive islanders well-nigh pass belief. These things are seldom proclaimed at home; they happen at the very ends of the earth; they are done in a corner, and there are none to reveal them. But there is, nevertheless, many a petty trader that has navigated the Pacific whose course from island to island might be traced by a series of cold-blooded robberies, kidnappings, and murders, the iniquity of which might be considered almost sufficient to send her guilty timbers to the bottom of the sea.

It was an Australian whaler, the *Lucy Ann*, that took Melville on. The captain had stopped at Nukahiva to recruit seamen because eight of his men had recently deserted and two others had been put in irons for threatening mutiny. Not a happy prospect. The captain allowed Herman to join the ship for just one cruise, until they reached the next port.

The *Lucy Ann* arrived at Tahiti in the Society Islands about six weeks later. Here too Herman saw the French flag flying, a recent takeover under threat of bombardment by a French warship in the harbor. He stayed only a few days, until he signed on to the *Charles and Henry*, a Nantucket whaleship that had sailed in, unhappy at bad luck in overfished waters. After an eight-month cruise it had stowed only 350 barrels of oil. Captain Coleman complained too that his boatsteerers were not the best in the world. Short of men, the captain signed Melville on, agreeing he need stay only for the next cruise. Around November 6, Melville went aboard with only what was on his back.

He was soon at ease with his shipmates. He proved to be, if not a great whaleman, a great storyteller. He had plenty of experience to start with, and an imagination that lifted the facts into the realm of art. The whalers were eager to find out: Were all island people cannibals? If not, what did they eat? Was everybody tattooed? And the girls, were they all as beautiful as some say?

Bad luck in sighting and capturing whales continued. It gave Melville plenty of time to read. This was one whaleship the Quaker owners had stocked liberally with books and magazines. Adventure, travel, history, biography. Fiction too, with *Robinson Crusoe* and *Gulliver's Travels* among Melville's favorites.

But of whaling? Little to report. Melville later claimed he had been a harpooner, though the records don't bear that out. If he had ever flung a harpoon at whales, it didn't impress the captain, for he lamented this was one voyage that lacked a single competent harpooner.

After six months at sea, the *Charles and Henry* anchored at Lahaina in the Hawaii Islands. The volcanic archipelago was first visited by Europeans in 1778, when Captain James Cook stopped there. Now the islands were ruled by King Kamehameha III. American traders for decades had been exploiting the islands' natural resources. It brought a degree of prosperity for some, but it also introduced disease, firearms, and liquor. A few years before Melville's arrival, Christian missionaries had begun to evangelize the native people.

As Melville had signed on only for the cruise, on May 2, 1843, he went ashore, a free man on the island of Maui. Lahaina was the chief seaport in Hawaii for whalers. It was a town of about three thousand, many of the people living in grass houses on a street lining the beach. In the last ten weeks

Honolulu was Melville's last taste of tropical life before joining the navy.

almost ninety whaleships had come into the port, most of them American, and a few from France, Canada, England, and Belgium. Mountain peaks reared as high as 6,000 feet (1,800 meters) beyond the shore, and bananas, tapas, and sugarcane were abundant.

Melville had seen what the Europeans had done to Tahiti. Now he saw what Americans were doing to another tropical paradise. Protestant missionaries were given a free hand by the king and one of them, G. P. Judd, was serving as prime minister.

Late in May, Melville took a schooner to nearby Honolulu, a town of about ten thousand people on the island of Oahu. There he would stay for three months. He found work as a pinsetter in one of its bowling alleys, and learned to bowl himself. But the pay was so low he quit and signed a contract to be a clerk for a merchant from New York who was opening a new store. The pay: $150 a year.

Soon he was selling calico across the counter at four yards for a dollar, busy as he had once been in the cap and fur store in Albany. He turned twenty-four on August 1, and a few days later the frigate *United States*, the flagship of the Pacific squadron, arrived in Honolulu. American seamen like Melville knew its reputation for speed and its historic role in the War of 1812.

When the sailors came ashore, they shared with Melville old hometown newspapers, and suddenly he was deep in thoughts of his family back home—his mother, his brothers, his sisters.

Overcome with homesickness, he gave up his dream of tropical life, and joined the navy.

CHAPTER 9

In The Navy

Onboard the *United States* as an ordinary seaman, Melville found himself amid sixteen times as many men as the *Acushnet* carried. Though the warship was only about twice as long as the whaler, she carried some 480 officers and men.

A few hours after Melville stepped on deck, all hands were called to witness official punishment on bare backs. The first sailor got twelve lashes for striking a sentry; the second, twelve for smuggling in liquor; the third and fourth, cabin boys, six lashes each for fighting and swearing. On the next day, three more men were given twelve lashes each for drunkenness.

You couldn't avoid watching the torturous treatment. Do it you must; that was the regulation. While he served on the *United States*, Melville would witness 150 floggings—in just fourteen months.

To divert himself from such grim happenings, Melville plowed through even more books aboard than on the whaleship. The frigate's library included the Harper's Family Library, a collection of seventy-two books, well chosen to both entertain and educate. The series included biography, history, travel, and scientific works too. One of these last was Charles Darwin's account of his 1835 voyage on the *Beagle* to the Galápagos, where Melville had been. The book was the nucleus of what would become Darwin's theory of evolution. The sailors read aloud to one another the poems and prose

The U.S.S. United States, *shown in the foreground, is anchored in Honolulu Harbor in August 1843, just before Melville boarded her for his time in the navy.*

they liked, and discussed the reports of naval battles some of them had fought in.

In *White-Jacket*, Melville's novel that would fictionalize his experience on the *United States*, he describes the men's hunger for reading:

> Just glance your eye along our ships' decks when lying in port; under the break of the poop you may observe a group of mizen-topmen, eagerly listening to some more talented shipmate, who, with voice and effect worthy [of] the subject, is reading aloud passages from one of the splendid and romantic poems of the celebrated Byron:—In the larboard gangway a crowd are assembled, distorting their risible muscles at the trying though ludicrous scenes in Marryatt's Jacob Faithful or Midshipman Easy:—Again, on the starboard side amongst the main-topmen, a little coterie are gathered together, wrapped in profound silence, every ear intent, with open mouth swallowing some of Cooper's

thrilling descriptions of nautical life, or digesting the eccentricities of Scott's liquor-loving Peter Pebbles, or the original and trite [sic] remarks of Boz's inimitable Sam Weller; and even the hard old salts on the forecastle, with the bronze of every climate upon their furrowed cheeks, are huddled together around the trunk, hearing, with enthusiastic imagination and eyes beaming with delight, some lettered "sheet-anchor-man" describe the glorious exploits and brilliant achievements of Columbia's ships in the last war.

Melville added that "the books that prove most agreeable, grateful and companionable are those that we pick up by chance here and there; those which seem put into our hands by Providence; those which pretend to little, but abound in much." (Not that there's anything wrong with the school or public library!)

In *White-Jacket*, published in 1850, Melville sticks pretty closely to facts. You learn that many foreigners as well as African-American slaves served in America's navy. Not unusual, for all countries at that time enlisted foreigners. Scholars have been able to pin down the true identity of several characters in the novel. Those Melville became close to were men with his love for literature. Melville could recite poems too, and he found again that he could tell stories in a way that entranced all his listeners.

Although this was not a time when the United States was at war, still sailors died. Melville watched one man buried at sea, and soon after, the ship's cooper was jerked overboard in a freakish accident and drowned. Another fell from the yard and broke an arm and a leg. And more would die as the frigate roved the ocean.

In late November, after cruising some 5,000 miles (8,000 kilometers), the frigate reached the Juan Fernández islands, off the coast of Chile. On one of these islands the Scottish sailor Alexander Selkirk had been put ashore in 1704 after a quarrel with his ship's captain. Somehow he survived four years and four months of complete isolation, before being rescued. It was a great adventure made famous when Daniel Defoe fictionalized the story in *Robinson Crusoe*.

After two weeks in the Chilean harbor of Valparaíso the ship sailed to Peru, and Melville had the chance to visit Lima, the capital, a three-hundred-year-old white city surrounded by lofty walls. He went into its Grand Cathedral, an awesome sight with its altar decorated in gold and jewels. Gruesome were the desiccated remains of many archbishops, visible in the open coffins of the cathedral. Later, in *Moby-Dick*, he describes his vision of the city:

> Nor is it, altogether, the remembrance of her cathedral-toppling earthquakes; nor the stampedoes of her frantic seas; nor the tearlessness of arid skies that never rain; nor the sight of her wide field of leaning spires, wrenched copestones, and crosses all adroop (like canted yards of anchored fleets); and her suburban avenues of house-walls lying over upon each other, as a tossed pack of cards;—it is not these things alone which made tearless Lima, the strangest, saddest city thou can'st see. For Lima has taken the white veil; and there is a higher horror in this whiteness of her woe. Old as Pizarro, this whiteness keeps her ruins for ever new; admits not the cheerful greenness of complete decay; spreads over her broken ramparts the rigid pallor of an apoplexy that fixes its own distortions.

Lima's magnificence and strangeness would haunt Melville's imagination. Much later he made the city the scene for one of his best tales, "The Town-Ho's Story" (chapter 54 in *Moby-Dick*) and used it as the setting for the ending of his short story "Benito Cereno."

While anchored off the coast of Peru, the ship's crew were day after day the victims or the witnesses of flogging after flogging.

A woodcut showing how the plaza and Grand Cathedral of Lima,
Peru, must have looked when Melville visited there.

After several weeks on Peru's coast, the *United States* sailed to Mazatlán, Mexico, then turned around and sailed back to Peru, where it stopped for some weeks before moving on to Rio de Janeiro in Brazil. It sounds like exciting travel, except that for whatever reason, Melville didn't go ashore all this while. It only underlines the fact that sailors may circle the globe, but see little besides water.

Sailing on the warship, Melville deepened his understanding of history and human behavior even more than on his merchant and whaling voyages. According to Melville's biographer Hershel Parker, out of the older sailors

> he drew stories of naval battles going far back into the 18th century, told . . . by men long dead . . . In reflecting on a man-of-war with its authoritarian discipline as a microcosm of western civilization, Melville clarified for himself the meaning of phases of pagan life as he had witnessed it, paradise found in the valley of the Typee, paradise lost in Tahiti, the landscape and seascape desecrated by commerce, the surviving Tahitians themselves ravaged by European diseases and deprived of their ancestral customs and religion by the missionaries. In Hawaii he had seen missionaries and their wives treat the Hawaiians more like slaves than converts. In the *United States*, living not under the Bill of Rights but under the Articles of War, he had ample time to assimilate his lessons in cultural relativity.

On August 24, 1844, Melville's ship left Rio for home. On October 3, it docked in the Charlestown Navy Yard, outside Boston. And on the 14th, seaman Herman Melville was discharged from the U.S. Navy.

What had been going on at home these nearly four years Melville had been away?

An 1843 watercolor depicting the flogging of a sailor aboard the navy ship U.S.S. Cyane.

Flogging

If you came aboard an American warship drunk, if you got into a scrap, if you disobeyed an order, if you sounded insolent, if you cursed, then you were due for a flogging. Corporal punishment was standard in the American military during the nineteenth century. But in the navy—where mutiny was feared—lashing was imposed for even the most trivial offense.

The victim's shirt was taken off, and he was tied at the ankles and wrists to a hatch covering. Usually it was the boatswain's mate who swung the cat-o'-nine-tails—a short-handled whip with nine knotted leather thongs.

Reports by witnesses or by the victims themselves assert this punishment left lifelong scarring. Not just physical, but emotional too. The moment of punishment could last a lifetime.

How could you not be driven wild at the lack of proportion between punishment and offense? The absence of trial, or the chance to appeal? The lashing of sailors but the exemption of officers? And the absolute godlike authority of the captain, acting as his own judge and jury?

How different, Melville asked, are these conditions from the treatment of slaves?

When Melville's *White-Jacket* was published in 1850, it added to growing public anger over flogging in the navy, which led to a congressional investigation. Not long after, Congress passed a law ending flogging in the navy.

One admiral, Samuel Franklin, said that Melville's book "had more influence in abolishing corporal punishment in the navy than anything else."

CHAPTER 10

First Book

When Melville came off the frigate he was once more a private citizen. Now twenty-five, he was handsome, bearded, deeply tanned, and with nothing of his own but a rich supply of seafaring yarns.

In all those years away from home, Herman seems to have heard little or nothing from his family. They, however, had received some of his letters, passed from ship to ship. He lingered in Boston for a while, visiting his Melvill aunts and his father's old friend, Lemuel Shaw. At the judge's handsome home on Beacon Hill he met Shaw's daughter, Elizabeth—called Liz—an attractive young woman of twenty-two, eager to hear his adventures. Liz no doubt could have married any of the Harvard graduates in her social circle. But this newcomer was far more fascinating, with his vivid tales of hunting great whales and living with cannibal tribes in tropical wonderlands.

From the Shaws and his aunts, Melville learned that his brothers Gansevoort and Allan were now practicing law in New York. And of course that his mother was waiting anxiously for him in Lansingburgh.

By boat and train Melville reached New York on October 19 and met Allan at his boardinghouse on Greenwich Street.

Gansevoort was not in town. He had become something of a celebrity. An ardent supporter of the Democratic party and its presidential candidate, James K. Polk, he had developed a flamboyant speaking style that delighted great crowds hungry for free entertainment. "The orator of the human race," they called him.

While at sea Melville had heard little of politics back home. He had much to catch up on. And Allan was eager to fill him in. Polk's party was all for expanding the nation, taking over the vast territories of California and the Southwest that now belonged to Mexico. While support for expansion could be found in all parts of the United States, the engine powering the movement was the southern plantation aristocracy. They hungered for more land that could be slave cultivated. It was America's Manifest Destiny, God's will, the propagandists of expansion proclaimed, that the United States should take possession of those vast regions. Even if it meant war with Mexico.

The abolitionists fought fiercely against the expansionists. Henry Clay, the Whig party's candidate, scared of Polk's popular appeal, walked a tightrope on the issue. In disgust with Clay's posture, the antislavery forces fielded their own candidate, James A. Birney, on the Liberty party ticket.

In New York, with its large Irish population, Gansevoort spoke out for Irish independence from Britain, which made him a hero to an important group of voters. He proved himself a masterful orator, and his party's leaders predicted a major role for him some day. He became so popular, said Allan, that, can you imagine! former presidents—John Quincy Adams, Martin Van Buren, Andrew Jackson—welcomed him into their homes!

After fitting out Melville with decent civilian clothing, Allan sent him up to Lansingburgh. There he found his mother looking much the same. His sisters and brothers were now all in their teens. They too couldn't get enough of his sea stories. But he soon felt restless, longing to see Gansevoort, the man who was making a great name for himself. The newspapers were printing his speeches—some three hours long—almost daily. Why couldn't he too become a "somebody"?

He was just in time to march in a huge Democratic parade on November 1, with twenty bands of musicians and 20,000 demonstrators carrying thousands of torches through the streets to City Hall Park. And there on horseback with the party leaders was Gansevoort, riding under the proud eyes of his brothers.

On election day, November 6, Polk would win a narrow victory over Clay. The votes that went for Birney and his antiwar, antislavery party were just enough to tip the balance in Polk's favor.

Soon after the election, Melville went back to Lansingburgh. In the first years he had been away his mother had at times been unable to meet daily expenses. And as usual, Uncle Peter Gansevoort had ignored requests for help. But when Melville's brothers began practicing law, they sent her money now and then.

It was time Melville decided what to do with his life. The family's dismal history in business was not encouraging. What profession was he fitted for? None that anyone could see. Except, except . . . telling great stories. One day either family or friend said, "Why don't you put in book form that story of your South Seas adventures which we all enjoy so much?"

He at once accepted the suggestion. After all, hadn't two of his pieces been published even before he made the first voyage to Liverpool? And now he had rich and exotic experiences to work with. Then too there was the success Dana won with his sea story.

Not that he could expect to make a decent living by writing. N. P. Willis, himself author and editor, had just printed a piece on "Authors Pay in America" that claimed the publisher got two to five times as much for each book as the author did. Still, getting your name in print might help pave the way to some other career.

During the winter of 1844–1845, Melville plunked himself down at a desk in the law office of his brothers on Nassau Street, and began to write *Typee*. He could get off to a good start with stories he had often told about life on the tropical island, improving on them each time. But he didn't rely solely on personal experience. He made use of books by others, voyagers themselves, some of them experts on the Marquesas Islands.

Months passed as he struggled to shape his first book. Meanwhile Gansevoort was pulling strings, seeking letters of recommendation from influential politicians in the hope of getting a good government job as a reward for his campaigning services.

Some sheets of Melville's first drafts survive, and they show what a scribbler he was. He could write clearly if he worked slowly and carefully. But when fresh ideas flowed through his mind, his hand quickened and the sentences could be almost unreadable. It meant he had to copy out the material carefully, if he hoped an editor would read it. Or more likely, since he couldn't afford to pay a copyist, get someone else to do it for him. A painful job that would fall to members of the family.

Into his draft Melville would sometimes insert thinly disguised references to members of his family. He got fun out of his sensuous description of the Polynesian girls because he knew it would make his four sisters feel uncomfortable. Later he would cut some of the teasing, for after all the book wasn't meant only for the family.

He had trouble deciding just who the book was meant for. Should he present himself (as Tom) in the role of an uneducated sailor, like most of his shipmates, a rough type whose observations and expressions would fit the reader's conception? In revising the draft he cut some, but not all, words, sentences, and paragraphs that might sound too learned, too high-toned.

While working on the book, Melville picked up some idea of the literary world centered in New York. The city, as

Dickens had viewed it on a recent visit, was a dirty, noisy, brutal marketplace, dominated by merchants and bankers. Washington Irving, William Cullen Bryant, and James Fenimore Cooper were the famous writers. New and younger writers, it was hoped, would help create a "big" national literature, because weren't we a big country?

Early that summer, Herman went up to his mother's home in Lansingburgh to complete work on the novel. Liz was there too, visiting with relatives, and they got to know one another better.

However much he labored to improve his writing, the final version contains some stock language and banal passages. At least in the eye of the modern reader, who usually comes to *Typee* after reading the great prose of *Moby-Dick*. What was best about his first novel was his sensitivity to the mysterious nature of human perceptions. Why do we see things the way we do? How do we understand what's in other people's minds?

With a clean copy of the manuscript ready, Herman took it to Harper and Brothers, the New York publisher. He believed it was a good bet for them, for they had published Dana's highly successful book, and wasn't *Typee* a seafaring story too? Besides, they had a good reputation for handsome design and strong promotion and sales.

When a Harper and Brothers reader finished the book, he reported it was just as good as *Robinson Crusoe,* and recommended publication. But Harper's rejected it on the ground that "it was impossible that it could be true and therefore was without real value." One of Melville's sisters reportedly said that Harper's refusing it "embittered his whole life."

If Harper's rejected *Typee*, Herman thought no one else would want it. What he had sweated over all those months was a waste of time. Disgusted and depressed, he packaged the manuscript in a bag and leaving it in his brothers' law office, went back to Lansingburgh. He shared a bleak mood with

Gansevoort, who was demoralized by President Polk's failure to reward him with a government job.

Then, unexpectedly, the State Department informed Gansevoort that he was appointed secretary of the American legation in London. Not much pay, but prestige and a step up the diplomatic ladder. While waiting to sail, Gansevoort was visited by a friend, Thomas Nichols, a Democratic journalist. One day, killing time in the law office, Nichols picked up the *Typee* manuscript and read it straight through in two hours. Delighted with the book, and sure it would please all readers, he urged Gansevoort to take it to London and seek a British publisher for it.

Gansevoort promised to do it, and he and Nichols earned Herman's deep gratitude. Later, after getting to know Herman, Nichols wrote, "He was a simple-hearted, enthusiastic man of genius, who wrote with the consciousness of an impelling force, and with great power and beauty."

What would a London publisher think?

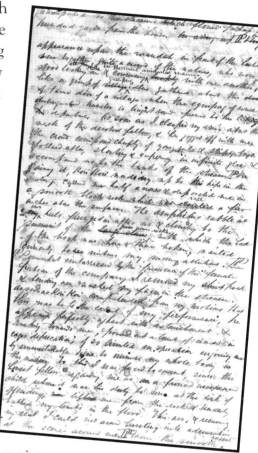

The original manuscript of Typee *as Melville wrote it in 1845 has been preserved on microfiche at the Gansevoort Library.*

CHAPTER 11

A Married Man

Nothing to do but wait. Wait to see if Gansevoort would find a London publisher for *Typee*. Months passed with Herman neither looking for a job nor starting work on another book. Somehow the family got by on what Allan Melville was able to send their mother.

Gansevoort took Herman's manuscript to the publisher John Murray. He liked it, and had the American author Washington Irving read it too. Irving's enthusiasm ensured publication. But first Herman had to agree to remove some passages Murray thought in bad taste, particularly those describing the dancing of the Marquesan girls. The contract paid Herman an advance of about $400 in return for the printing of one thousand copies. That sum was enough to support a small American family for about half a year.

Wiley & Putnam, a New York house, agreed to issue *Typee* on this side of the Atlantic in March 1846. From here on, Herman's books would follow this pattern: out first in London, then reprinted in New York. The British press was delighted with the book's blend of paganism and sophistication.

Many American reviewers liked it too. A New York magazine called it "one of the most interesting, amusing, and original books of adventure."

The book's editor, Evert A. Duyckink, sent Nathaniel Hawthorne a copy of the book, and the highly respected novelist wrote a warm review (unsigned) for his Salem newspaper:

The book is lightly but vigorously written; and we are acquainted with no work that gives a freer and more effective picture of barbarian life, in that unadulterated state of which there are now so few specimens remaining. The gentleness of disposition that seems akin to the delicious climate, is shown in contrast with traits of savage fierceness;—on one page, we read of manners and modes of life that indicate a whole system of innocence and peace; and on the next, we catch a glimpse of a smoked human head, and the half-picked skeleton of what had been (in a culinary sense) a well-dressed man. The author's descriptions of the native girls are voluptuously colored, yet not more so than the exigencies of the subject appear to require. He has that freedom of view—it would be too harsh to call it laxity of principle—which renders him tolerant of codes of morals that may be little in accordance with our own; a spirit proper enough to a young and adventurous sailor, and which makes his book the more wholesome to our staid landsmen.

Walt Whitman, then editor of the Brooklyn *Eagle*, called *Typee* "a strange, graceful, most readable book. . . . As a book to pore dreamily over of a summer day, it is unsurpassed."

But before Gansevoort could do more to advance Herman's career, he was dead. On May 12, 1846, the eldest son, the family pride, gone at thirty-one. He had long been in poor health, but no one expected so early an end. Before the terrible news reached Herman, he wrote his brother a letter full of joy over the book's success and noting too that Americans "are all in a state of delirium" about the war with Mexico that President Polk had just proclaimed. "Who knows what all this may lead to?" And warning that the killed and wounded "will be reckoned up by thousands."

Now Herman, who never wished it, was head of the family, with his mother and sisters to live with him. No one had expected him ever to replace Gansevoort; he could barely support himself. For years he had sailed the world's oceans, unable

Nathaniel Hawthorne and Melville, both destined to be regarded as the literary giants of their era, became friends while Hawthorne was in his forties and Melville still in his twenties.

to send a dollar to help his mother, four sisters, and two younger brothers. With Gansevoort gone, and *Typee* published, he was only beginning to create himself. Later he would tell his new friend Nathaniel Hawthorne that until he was twenty-five, he had had no development at all. And suddenly he must leap into full maturity, and responsibility for a large family.

Herman was not yet done with resisting attempts to censor *Typee*. Duyckink had to tell him that the company demanded a drastic cutting of certain passages in the American edition, those criticizing the missionary actions in the islands. It was hard to consent, but intensely eager to see *Typee* published, he agreed to do it in such a way that would not harm "the general character and style of the book."

Then from John Murray in London came a letter telling Melville he would like to publish his next book, as a sequel to *Typee*. Great news! So promising that Herman felt he could now propose to Liz Shaw. And she happily accepted him, for wasn't his future as a successful writer assured?

They became engaged in 1846, even though Judge Shaw wasn't so confident about Herman's future. Perhaps he suggested that his future son-in-law apply for a patronage job, a path old Major Gansevoort, the hero of the Boston Tea Party, had taken. So in February 1847, Herman went down to Washington, armed with letters of recommendation. His hunt failed, and he returned home. Disappointed? Or probably relieved not to be tied to a desk doing dull chores all day long.

What about lecturing as a way to earn easy money? He had already been invited to a public platform, but had turned down the offer, though he knew how great a storyteller he was. Foolish, for it would have helped build a more solid base for marriage.

Instead, he turned to book reviewing for supplementary income. Sometimes he did it for free, other times for the small sums editors paid.

Herman and Liz were married in Boston in August 1847. They honeymooned in New Hampshire. He was twenty-eight, she was twenty-five. She was charming, agreeable, and girlish in the way of young women of the upper class, with fair complexion and regular features. She had fallen for the handsome sailor almost as soon as he began telling his tales in the family parlor. Neither of them knew how troubling an artist's life could be, how unromantic the relentless drive to create works no public was clamoring for. Liz would raise two sons and two daughters, suffer the tragic early loss of two of them, and endure the long years of Herman's creative pain and disappointments. Not to mention the exhausting labor of copying his manuscripts.

Without waiting to see *Typee* published, Herman began writing a sequel in the winter of 1846–1847. He had much more to tell about his voyaging and wrote rapidly. He titled the book *Omoo*—a Polynesian word meaning "rover"—and called the character telling the story "Typee."

In *Omoo* and several of the books that followed *Typee*, Melville continued to draw upon his experiences at sea. The

Elizabeth Shaw Melville and Herman Melville in 1847, the year of their marriage.

seven books published between 1846 and 1852 portray people from various races and classes. Reading them gives you the broad range of Herman's interests, his sympathy for others, his anxieties about the conflicts he encounters. In writing the novels he was inevitably shaped by his own family's history and by the society he grew up in.

What dominated his age was the issue of race and slavery. But he was not blind to what white working people endured. In *Typee* and *Omoo* we look at what government and missionaries did to native peoples. In *Redburn*, at poverty in England. In *White-Jacket*, at abuses in the U.S. Navy. In *Israel Potter*, at the betrayal of American Revolutionary ideals. In his short stories, at the smugness of the rich and the exploitation of the working class.

When his personal experience did not suffice, he enriched his stories with knowledge and insights gathered from other books. In all his fiction, a quest, a search of some kind is the connecting thread: for the primal nature of men and women

No Way to Get Rich

About a year after publication of *Typee,* a financial report from Putnam showed that some 1,200 copies of the book had been sold, producing $661.94 of income. The publisher had deducted expenses of $439.18, leaving Herman with $111.38. But deduct from that the $103.57 Herman was charged for buying copies for his own use, and he was left with $7.81.

No way to get rich, this author's life. Nor did most other authors do better. Only two—Washington Irving and James Fenimore Cooper—were said to earn enough from their books for a family to live on. The others—including such famous names as Emerson, Thoreau, Whittier, Longfellow, Bryant, and Hawthorne—had family money, or a professorship, or an editor's or journalist's or clerk's job to depend on.

in *Typee* and *Omoo,* for a dream girl in *Mardi,* for a father in *Redburn,* for home in *White-Jacket.* And as for *Moby-Dick,* more on this later.

Despite his passionate indictment of the world's cruelties, Melville in *Moby-Dick* could still say this about humanity:

> Men may seem detestable as joint-stock-companies and nations; knaves, fools, and murderers there may be; men may have mean and meager faces; but man, in the ideal, is so noble and sparkling, such a grand and glowing creature, that over any ignominious blemish in him all his fellows should run to throw their costliest robes. . . . Humanity, thou strong thing, I worship thee, not in the laureled victor, but in this vanquished one.

CHAPTER 12

More Children and More Books

Although Harper's had rejected *Typee*, Herman tried them with *Omoo*. To his surprise, they accepted it at once. Author and publisher would go 50-50 on profits, after Harper's had recovered the costs of publication.

Where would the new couple live, and Herman work? Liz did not want to move in with Herman's family in Lansingburgh. Judge Shaw generously solved the problem with his gift of a house in New York City.

It was a big brownstone, at 103 Fourth Avenue, just behind Grace Church and near Union Square. There both Herman and Liz, together with his newlywed brother Allan and his wife, Sophia, plus their mother and sisters, would live.

There was lots of space for everyone, with Herman having his own workroom. The family had breakfast around 8 A.M., then Herman took a walk while Liz straightened out his workroom. Returning, he would write till lunch at 12:30, and then be back at his desk till dinnertime. After that, he and Liz would talk for an hour, or he might read to her what he'd written that day. Then another walk for Herman, and around 8 P.M. the family would gather in the parlor while one of them would read aloud to the others. Bedtime was 10 for everyone.

Omoo came out that year to good reviews but also fierce attacks by the conservative religious press. Herman was having a fine time, popular with hostesses of the salon set. Then too there were Duyckink's Saturday night dinners, where literary friends debated political and cultural issues over brandy and cigars. It was so joyful a time that he told Duyckink, "I wish to God Shakespeare had lived later, and promenaded in Broadway."

Not much money was coming in, however. Maintaining a big house with a big family was expensive, and Herman and Allan worried constantly over paying the bills. Herman began his next book, *Mardi*, as soon as he'd read the proofs of *Omoo*. Again he made the narrator an American sailor deserting a whaling expedition. His driving impulse was to create a book popular with female readers, who did most of the book buying. The result, published by Richard Bentley in London and Harper's in New York, was a romance "wild enough" he hoped to please that audience.

It didn't reach them, for the book drew poor reviews, which meant poor sales. Some critics called it "unintelligible and tedious," and one even labeled it "trash."

About the time *Mardi* appeared, Herman and Liz had their first child, Malcolm. The new father was ecstatic. The child "is a perfect prodigy," he told his brother Allan. "Who would have thought that the birth of one little man, when ten thousands of other little men; 8 little horses, 8 little guinea pigs & little roosters; & the Lord only knows what, are being born— that the birth of one little phenomenon should create such a panic thro' the world: nay, even in heaven; for last night I dreamt that his good angel had secured a seat for him above; & that the Devil roared terribly bethinking him of the lusty foe to sin born into this sinful world."

The Melvilles would have three more children: Stanwix born in 1851, Elizabeth in 1853, and Frances in 1855. Except

The Melville children as photographed in 1861, from left: Malcolm, Elizabeth, Frances, and Stanwix.

for the last child, their futures would not be happy. Malcolm was a suicide at eighteen; Stanwix died of tuberculosis at thirty-five; Elizabeth was crippled with rheumatoid arthritis and remained at home, unmarried, in her mother's care. Frances was the only one to thrive, marrying well and having daughters and granddaughters who would care for Melville's legacy.

To have a child was wonderful. Not to have the income to support your family, that was frightening enough to make any man, writer or not, tense with worry. When *Mardi* failed with reviewers and readers alike, Herman decided he must shape his "product" for the marketplace. The result was two adventure stories, *Redburn* (1849) and *White-Jacket* (1850). "They are two *jobs*," he wrote his father-in-law, "which I have done for money—being forced to it, as other men are to sawing wood."

As authors sometimes do, he minimized what his true accomplishment was in both these books. A biographer, Elizabeth Hardwick, has called *Redburn* "one of the most appealing and certainly the most personal of his works." And she goes on to say how *Redburn* in its opening pages offers "a profoundly moving poem to his dead father":

> I had learned to think much and bitterly before my time . . .
> talk not of the bitterness of middle-age and after life; a boy
> can feel all that and much more, when upon his young soul
> the mildew has fallen; and the fruit, which with others is
> only blasted after ripeness, with him is nipped in the first
> blossom and bud. And never again can such blights be made
> good; they strike too deep, and leave such a scar that the air
> of Paradise might not erase it.

As Redburn watches emigrants boarding his ship for America, he thinks, "You cannot spill a drop of American blood without spilling the blood of the whole world. . . . Our blood is as the flood of the Amazon, made up of a thousand currents all pouring into one. We are not a nation, so much as a world."

Commenting on such passages, the critic Philip Rahv credits Melville for "an extraordinarily moving celebration of the hopes lodged in the New World and one of the noblest pleas in our literature for the extinction of national hatreds and racial prejudice."

What was happening in Melville's America made him at times write as a social reformer. In the 1840s a nativist movement sprang up, fired by anti-Catholic prejudice and the Irish immigration of the potato famine years. The nativists took political action to try to deny the right to vote to Catholics and the foreign born. It led to bloody riots in the streets and even the burning of convents. Herman was infuriated by it, and in *Redburn* wrote:

> Let us waive that agitated national topic, as to whether
> multitudes of foreign poor should be landed on our
> American shores; let us waive it, with the one only thought,
> that if they can get here, they have God's right to come;
> though they bring all Ireland and her miseries with them.
> For the whole world is the patrimony of the whole world;
> there is no telling who does not own a stone in the Great
> Wall of China.

With the same speed Herman wrote *Redburn*, he finished *White-Jacket* in sixty days. To him this was slave labor, and he never boasted about how hard he'd pushed himself. He used his own experience on his voyage home from the Pacific on the frigate. *White-Jacket* is both the title of the book and the nickname of the narrator because he always wears the white duck outfit that was navy issue. Herman again drew on many reference books to flesh out the story.

He made life on a warship stand for life in the everyday world, when so gross an injustice as slavery is tolerated. The powerful who order the flogging are the symbol of man's inhumanity to man.

The novel reads too as a book about work, about holding a job and what a man does for it and what it does to him. It celebrates the warmth, the intimacy, the comradeship that pulling together on a common project can create.

Harper's agreed to publish the book and advanced him $500. A British publisher might pay him even more; why not go to London himself to seek a deal? The energy put into these last two books had been exhausting. A sea voyage would restore him. However, he was nursing the idea for another book, based on an old pamphlet about the strange life of Israel Potter, an American of his grandfather's time who after the Revolution lived in exile in England. Every journey seemed to fill his mind with observations and information that would find their way into a book.

While he was gone the four months, Liz and little Malcolm went up to Boston to stay with Judge Shaw. She won't mind our separation so much, Herman told himself, because she'd have lots of family and friends around her.

In October 1849 he crossed the Atlantic in a sailing ship. A celebrity now, he was given the best cabin, a great contrast with his voyage to Liverpool ten years ago! Unable to resist showing off to the passengers, he climbed to the ship's masthead and played around in the rigging awhile.

The fun didn't last; publisher after publisher turned down *White-Jacket*. In between appointments, he filled the days and weeks with sightseeing. A gruesome moment was witnessing, with 30,000 others, the public hanging of a husband and wife convicted of murder. "Horrible, unspeakable," he noted in his journal. He visited art galleries, scoured the bookstores, dropped in on houses and taverns linked to great writers.

Late in November he crossed to France to visit Paris. Then on to Belgium and Germany and back to Britain. As he prepared to return home, the publisher Bentley, who had lost money on *Mardi*, relented and agreed to do *White Jacket*.

Reviews of the American edition of *White-Jacket* had begun to appear. One of them remarked that the excitable youngster who wrote the earlier books had grown into a thoughtful man. Another said his treatment of character was genuinely Shakespearean. The first edition sold out quickly.

When Herman reached home at the end of January 1850, he found the whole family at their Fourth Avenue house, eager to see their wandering pilgrim. He distributed gifts to everyone.

And then settled in to begin writing *Moby-Dick*.

CHAPTER 13

Writing Moby-Dick

How did he write *Moby-Dick*?

It seems Herman began the book in New York early in 1850. In May he wrote Dana he was halfway through the story: "It will be a strange sort of book, tho', I fear; blubber is blubber you know; tho' you may get oil out of it, the poetry runs hard as sap from a frozen maple tree; & to cook the thing one must needs throw in a little fancy. . . . Yet I mean to give the truth of the thing, spite of this. . . ."

Late in June he proposed the work in progress to the British publisher Bentley, describing it as "a romance founded upon certain wild legends in the southern Sperm Whale Fisheries," and assuring him the book would use his own experience of two years or more as a whaleman.

Adding to his own would be the many sensational tales of hunts for whales picked up from shipmates and from crews he met in the ports of the Pacific. One was the *Essex* disaster, when the great white whale smashed headlong into that ship, and sank it. He had often heard of the mythic hunt for Mocha Dick, an old bull whale whose deviltry was notorious. For facts about the whaling industry he drew upon many published sources.

The style of writing that emerged was shaped by close reading of the Bible, especially the Book of Job and the Book of Jonah, and the classics of English and European literature. Not only Shakespeare, but Marlowe, Milton, Coleridge, Sterne, Dante, and Goethe.

Much of the work on the book would be done in the Berkshires. He had come to love the region through frequent visits to his Uncle Thomas's farm, outside Pittsfield. No longer content to work in Fourth Avenue, he decided to move the family to the Berkshires. With a loan from Judge Shaw of about half the cost, and taking out a mortgage, he bought a farm of 150 acres (60 hectares) and a house, paying $6,500 for them. By October 1850 they were in their new home, named Arrowhead because some ancient Indian relics had been turned up when the soil had been first plowed. Now Herman had added farming to his career.

Certainly Nathaniel Hawthorne was one reason for moving to the Berkshires. When the two first met in 1850, the year Hawthorne's most famous work, *The Scarlet Letter,* appeared, they had long and intimate conversations. Herman recognized in him a writer willing to confess the dark truths about human nature that Melville was just beginning to explore. Herman's dedication of *Moby-Dick* would read: "In token of my admiration for his genius this book is inscribed to Nathaniel Hawthorne." It was one of the few close friendships of Herman's life, inspiring at this critical time, but later, disappointing. For the two novelists were far apart on some crucial issues, such as slavery. Hawthorne in a presidential campaign biography of his college classmate Franklin Pierce had written that southern masters and their black slaves "dwelt together in greater peace and affection than had ever elsewhere existed between the taskmaster and the serf." Later, Hawthorne would say that it was "sentimental nonsense to risk American lives in order to liberate slaves."

That December, after settling in at Arrowhead, Melville wrote his friend and editor Duyckink of life on the farm:

I have a sort of sea-feeling here in the country, now that the ground is all covered with snow. I look out of my window in the morning when I rise as I would out of a port-hole of a ship in the Atlantic. My room seems a ship's cabin; & at nights when I wake up & hear the wind shrieking, I almost fancy there is too much sail on the house, & I had better go on the roof & rig in the chimney.

Do you want to know how I pass my time?—I rise at eight—thereabouts—& go to my barn—say good morning to the horse, & give him his breakfast. (It goes to my heart to give him a cold one, but it can't be helped.) Then, pay a visit to my cow—cut up a pumpkin or two for her, & stand by to see her eat it—for it's a pleasant sight to see a cow move her jaws—she does it so mildly & with such a sanc-tity.—My own breakfast over, I go to my work-room & light my fire—then spread my m.s.s. on the table,—take one business squint at it, & fall to with a will. At 2 1/2 P.M. I hear a preconcerted knock at my door, which (by request) continues till I rise and go to the door, which serves to wean me effectively from my writing, however interested I may be. My friends the horse & cow now demand their dinner— & I go & give it them. My own dinner over, I rig my sleigh & with my mother or sisters start off for the village—& if it be a *Literary World* day, great is the satisfaction thereof.— My evenings I spend in a sort of mesmeric state in my room—not being able to read—only now & then skimming over some large-printed book. . . .

Working on the book, often by candlelight, overstrained his eyes. In childhood an infection had damaged his vision, and as he grew older, the condition worsened. Obsessed with the need to finish the book, he drove on, reaching deep into his imagination for the mysteries of human nature. He began to believe he was achieving the quality of Shakespearean drama, grappling with universal themes.

Not that he copied Shakespeare. Rather, as one critic said, he did what Shakespeare in the nineteenth century might

Arrowhead, the Melville family farm, as photographed from the north field in about 1862.

have done with America and the sea. He made use of dramatic elements such as the soliloquy, the fool, comic byplay, asides, meditation. It isn't always done well, but it enriched the writing of novels as no American writer before him had done.

Although sure he was creating something great, he was far from feeling calm or content. For by this time, the summer of 1851, he was deeply in debt, owing more than $10,000. Happily, Bentley came through with an offer to publish the book in Britain, despite having lost money on the three previous books.

When Harper's refused to do an American edition, saying Melville owed them too much money, he decided to have the book printed at his own expense, and then to sell the printing plates to whatever publisher made the best offer. This, although he had not yet written the ending.

Every day he mixed farmwork with reading proofs, correcting, revising, and struggling to compose the ending. This book had to make money, or his career as a novelist would be ended, and Arrowhead, his family home, snatched away.

Then, in September, Harper's decided to do the book, using the plates Herman had paid for. The book appeared in England as *The Whale*, and in America as *Moby-Dick*, dedicated to Nathaniel Hawthorne. By a sad coincidence, on the eve of the book's publication, the press carried a sensational report of the sinking in the Pacific of the whaleship *Ann Alexander*, rammed by a huge sperm whale.

CHAPTER 14

————◆————

Melville's Voice

Melville wrote *Moby-Dick* at a time when the United States was pushing its people and its power to the far shores of the Pacific. Just as pioneers were opening up the West, Melville's novels were opening the oceans.

While the general tone of American writing was optimistic, Melville's outlook, like Hawthorne's, was darker. He saw horrors beneath the surface of the sea, and darkness in the human heart. He began *Moby-Dick* as another semiautobiographical account, but as his imagination soared, he focused the story on the quest for the White Whale.

Ishmael, his narrator, speaks in Melville's voice. What the reader feels in *Moby-Dick*, says the editor Charles Feidelson Jr., are "primal patterns of conflict between man and nature, between the glory and madness of the warrior-hero, between the malevolence and the providential guidance of all that lies beyond man."

The story grows out of the character of Ahab, the *Pequod's* captain, driven to madness in his pursuit of that other principal character, Moby Dick, the whale that crippled him, and his interaction with the men in the crew.

Here is Ahab, as Ishmael first sees him on the deck of the *Pequod*:

> As I mounted to the deck at the call of the forenoon watch, so soon as I leveled my glance toward the taffrail, forebod-

ing shivers ran over me. Reality outran apprehension; Captain Ahab stood upon his quarter-deck.

There seemed no sign of common bodily illness about him, nor of the recovery from any. He looked like a man cut away from the stake, when the fire has overrunningly wasted all the limbs without consuming them, or taking away one particle from their compacted aged robustness. His whole high, broad form, seemed made of solid bronze, and shaped in an unalterable mould, like Cellini's cast Perseus. Threading its way out from among his grey hairs, and continuing right down one side of his tawny scorched face and neck, till it disappeared in his clothing, you saw a slender rod-like mark, lividly whitish. It resembled that perpendicular seam sometimes made in the straight, lofty trunk of a great tree, when the upper lightning tearingly darts down it, and without wrenching a single twig, peels and grooves out the bark from top to bottom, ere running off into the soil, leaving the tree still greenly alive, but branded. Whether that mark was born with him, or whether it was the scar left by some desperate wound, no one could certainly say. . . .

So powerfully did the whole grim aspect of Ahab affect me, and the livid brand which streaked it, that for the first few moments I hardly noted that not a little of this overbearing grimness was owing to the barbaric white leg upon which he partly stood. It had previously come to me that this ivory leg had at sea been fashioned from the polished bone of the sperm whale's jaw. . . .

I was struck with the singular posture he maintained. Upon each side of the *Pequod*'s quarter deck, and pretty close to the mizen shrouds, there was an auger hole, bored about half an inch or so, into the plank. His bone leg steadied in that hole; one arm elevated, and holding by a shroud; Captain Ahab stood erect, looking straight out beyond the ship's ever-pitching prow. There was an infinity of firmest fortitude, a determinate, unsurrenderable wilfulness, in the fixed and fearless, forward dedication of that glance. Not a word he spoke; nor did his officers say aught to him; though by all their minutest gestures and expressions, they plainly showed the uneasy, if not painful, consciousness of being under a troubled master-eye. And not only that, but moody stricken Ahab stood before them with a crucifixion in his face; in all the nameless regal overbearing dignity of some mighty woe. . . .

It's impossible to condense the story of *Moby-Dick*. But perhaps these few passages will offer some sense of what Melville's writing is like. Here is how he describes the great whale's head, a battering ram:

You observe that in the ordinary swimming position of the Sperm Whale, the front of his head presents an almost wholly vertical plane to the water; you observe that the lower part of that front slopes considerably backwards, so as to furnish more of a retreat for the long socket which receives the boom-like lower jaw; you observe that the mouth is entirely under the head, much in the same way, indeed, as though your own mouth were entirely under your chin. Moreover you observe that the whale has no external nose; and that what nose he has—his spout hole—is on top of his head; you observe that his eyes and ears are at the sides of his head, nearly one third of his entire length from the front. Wherefore, you must now have perceived that the front of the Sperm Whale's head is a dead, blind wall, without a single organ or tender prominence of any sort whatsoever. Furthermore, you are now to consider that only in the extreme, lower, backward sloping part of the front of the head, is there the slighted vestige of bone; and not till you get near twenty feet from the forehead do you come to the full cranial development. So that this whole enormous boneless mass is as one wad. Finally, though, as will soon be revealed, its contents partly comprise the most delicate oil; yet, you are now to be apprised of the nature of the substance which so impregnably invests all that apparent effem-

*O*ver the years, the confrontation between Captain Ahab and the great white whale has been a favorite scene for illustrators. Man vs. Whale is a moment of visual as well as literary drama.

inacy. In some previous place I have described to you how the blubber wraps the body of the whale, as the rind wraps an orange. Just so with the head; but with this difference: about the head this envelope, though not so thick, is of a boneless toughness, inestimable by any man who had not handled it. The severest pointed harpoon, the sharpest lance darted by the strongest human arm, impotently rebounds from it. It is as though the forehead of the Sperm Whale were paved with horses' hoofs. I do not think that any sensation lurks in it. . . .

And the final selection. The destruction of the whaleship by Moby Dick:

From the ship's bows, nearly all the seamen now hung inactive; hammers, bits of plank, lances, and harpoons, mechanically retained in their hands, just as they had darted from their various employments; all their enchanted eyes intent upon the whale, which from side to side strangely vibrating his predestinating head, sent a broad band of overspreading semicircular foam before him as he rushed. Retribution, swift vengeance, eternal malice were in his whole aspect, and spite of all that mortal man could do, the solid white buttress of his forehead smote the ship's starboard bow, till men and timbers reeled. Some fell flat upon their faces. Like dislodged trucks, the head of the harpooneers aloft shook on their bull-like necks. Through the breach, they heard the waters pour, as mountain torrents down a flume. . . .

Diving beneath the settling ship, the whale ran quivering along its keel; but turning under water, swiftly shot to the surface again, far off the other bow, but within a few yards of Ahab's boat, where, for a time, he lay quiescent:

"I turn my body from the sun. What ho, Tashtego! let me hear thy hammer. Oh! Ye three unsurrendered spires of mine; thou uncracked keel; and only god-bullied hull, thou firm deck, and haughty helm, and Pole-pointed prow,—death-glorious ship! must ye then perish, and without me?

Am I cut off from the last fond pride of meanest ship-wrecked captains? Oh, lonely death on lonely life! Oh, now I feel my topmost greatness lies in my topmost grief. Ho, ho! from all your furthest bounds, pour ye now in, ye bold billows of my whole foregone life, and top this one piled comber of my death! Towards thee I roll, thou all-destroying but unconquering whale; to the last I grapple with thee; from hell's heart I stab at thee; for hate's sake I spit my last breath at thee. Sink all coffins and all hearses to one common pool! and since neither can be mine, let me then tow to pieces, while still chasing thee, though tied to thee, thou damned whale! Thus, I give up the spear!"

The harpoon was darted; the stricken whale flew forward; with igniting velocity the line ran through the groove;—ran foul. Ahab stooped to clear it; he did clear it; but the flying turn caught him round the neck, and voicelessly as Turkish mutes bowstring their victim, he was shot out of the boat, ere the crew knew he was gone. Next instant, the heavy eye-splice in the rope's final end flew out of the stark-empty tub, knocked down an oarsman, and smiting the sea, disappeared in its depths.

For an instant, the tranced boat's crew stood still; then turned. "The ship? Great God, where is the ship?" Soon they through dim, bewildering mediums saw her sidelong fading phantom, as in the gaseous Fata Morgana; only the uppermost masts out of water; while fixed by infatuation, or fidelity, or fate, to their once lofty perches, the pagan harpooneers still maintained their sinking lookouts on the sea. And now, concentric circles seized the lone boat itself, and all its crew, and each floating oar, and every lance-pole, and spinning, animate and inanimate, all round and round in one vortex, carried the smallest chip of the *Pequod* out of sight.

CHAPTER 15

The Years After

What Melville's *Moby-Dick* signifies has been interpreted in many ways. Readers then, as now, hold contradictory views. (You can decide for yourself what this wild and wonderful book means.)

When the novel was published in 1851, Melville was thirty-two. Many of the reviews were favorable. One critic saw in the novel "a pregnant allegory, intended to illustrate the mystery of human life." Another said the White Whale embodies "the vaster moral evil of the world." A British critic held that Ahab represents "the first supreme characterization of despair in western literature." The book was admired for "its bold and graphic sketches." What bothered some was its mixture of forms and types. They couldn't pigeonhole the novel, and that made them uncomfortable. A southern writer called the book "sad stuff, and dreary or ridiculous."

Though Melville owed Harper's money on his advance for *Moby-Dick*, they paid him $500 for his next book, *Pierre*. That novel, however, was a failure, attacked widely by the reviewers. "Trash . . . muddy . . . foul . . . corrupt . . ." were some of the arrows that wounded. One paper even headlined, "Herman Melville Crazy." Its hero is an aristocrat, and the fate Melville gave him shocked American morality. Melville, unwilling to give in to the narrow-minded, declared, "I write precisely as I please."

In the three years between *Pierre* and his next novel, *Israel Potter*, Melville wrote several stories for *Putnam's*, a magazine that paid well but went bankrupt. Among the pieces are "Bartleby, the Scrivener," "The Encantadas," and "Benito Cereno," which were collected in *Piazza Tales*.

When neither *Moby-Dick* nor *Pierre* sold well, Melville was bitterly disappointed. The family, always worried about money, saw no relief ahead. Worn to the bone by ceaseless labor at his writing desk, he must have been nervous, touchy, bad-tempered at times. Anyone in such a prolonged state is hard to live with.

As the 1850s wore on, Melville's hope dimmed that Americans would gradually realize the dream of freedom and equality for all embodied in the Declaration of Independence. In his novels he tried to overcome his readers' racism and to lead them to identify with all victims of oppression, regardless of color. But the passage of the Fugitive Slave Law of 1850 and the rulings of the courts (including his father-in-law's) to force runaway slaves back into bondage plunged him into a gloomy hopelessness.

He suffered severe attacks of rheumatism and sciatica, and was close to collapse, emotionally as well as physically. Believing that he needed some sort of steady employment, his family and friends tried, but failed, to have him appointed a U.S. consul. The family became so alarmed at his state of mind that they urged him to get away from it all and travel abroad. Judge Shaw, generous as always, paid for a tour of England, the Continent, and the Near East that kept him away from the fall of 1856 to the spring of 1857.

On his return home, Melville tried lecturing as a source of income. In the next three years he would travel and talk for pay. In the Northeast, the Midwest, and the South. It earned him little, and his career as a lecturer dried up.

In the winter of 1855–1856, Melville did manage to write one more novel, *The Confidence-Man,* and to get it published in 1857. His ninth book, it explores several of the themes taken up in earlier works. It takes place on a Mississippi riverboat headed for New Orleans, the financial headquarters of the cotton kingdom and the slaveholders who dominated the nation's government. Melville savages American con men, exposing their deceits and disguises, and indicts money madness as the betrayer of the national dream of freedom and equality.

No sooner was the novel out than the Panic of 1857 drove the publisher into bankruptcy. The book, a critical and commercial failure, turned out to be Melville's farewell to fiction.

In 1860, when his brother Tom, captain of the merchant clipper ship *Meteor,* returned to Boston Harbor, he suggested that Melville sail around the world with him as passenger. He hoped this might restore Herman's health. Liz and the four children would have to get along somehow on what her father could give her. But the ship never made it around the globe. Business plans were altered when they reached San Francisco, and Melville turned back alone to New York, not much benefited by the voyage.

CHAPTER 16

"What Unlike Things"

Home in November, Melville learned that a volume of poetry he had written had failed to find a publisher. Always a lover of poetry, reading it aloud, memorizing it, he would continue to write poetry for the rest of his life.

This was late in 1860, when Lincoln had just been elected president on a platform that opposed the extension of slavery. With the South threatening to secede, a civil war seemed inevitable. Melville himself didn't believe, as some of his family did, that if you left the issue alone, slavery would gradually disappear. "Only by agonized violence" would slavery be destroyed, he said.

In his forties, and head of a large family, he was too old to fight. Deeply affected by the war, he expressed his torn emotions in *Battle-Pieces*, published in 1866 by Harper's. In seventy-two poems, all of them short, many of them vivid pictures of combat, he portrayed the war as a tragedy of history.

The poems indicate how Melville had fallen away from the passionate opposition to racism expressed in his earlier works. Although war heroes are portrayed in the poems, none are African Americans, despite ample reports of their great courage under fire. About 200,000 blacks fought in the U.S. Army and Navy, and many thousands more did all kinds of work in support of the Union cause. They are missing from Melville's portrait of the war. In effect, his *Battle-Pieces* offers the four-year-struggle as a white man's war.

As the war ended, the nation debated what policy should be followed toward the defeated South. Just before *Battle-Pieces* went to press, late in 1866, Melville added a "Supplement" in prose. His political essay was meant to influence federal decisions on Reconstruction. He sided with President Andrew Johnson's pro-Confederate program, strongly opposed by the Radical Republicans in Congress. Although he denounced slavery as the basic cause of the war, Melville was against giving civil rights to the blacks while excluding Confederates from office. He had come to believe (as Lincoln and others had) that blacks and whites could not coexist peacefully in the South. He wanted the government to go slow in giving the former slaves the vote, while speeding up the restoration of civil rights to white southerners. His antiracist vision of earlier times had faded.

That essay was the end of Melville's political action. Just as *Battle-Pieces* was the end of his life as a professional author. He never intervened in politics again, or tried to influence public opinion.

Many critics judged that Melville was no poet, and *Battle-Pieces* sold less than five hundred copies. Yet today literary critics hold he was nineteenth-century America's leading poet, after Walt Whitman and Emily Dickinson.

In 1876, ten years after the Civil War poems, Melville at the family's expense published *Clarel,* a narrative poem that grew out of his travels in the Middle East in 1856–1857. It was bigger than anything he had done before, and took longer to write. Clarel is a student who explores the Holy Land in a quest for the source of faith. The huge poem of some 18,000 lines expresses, said one critic, Melville's "vision of a humanity that has lost a sense of conviction and is seeking to regain it."

During the war he went down to Washington once again to seek appointment to a consulate, and again was refused. Nor would the navy accept his offer to serve in some capacity.

In the fall of 1863 the family swapped Arrowhead for the house of Melville's brother Allan, at 104 East 26th Street, in New York. There Melville would live for the rest of his life. It was a brick townhouse with Melville's book-lined study on the second floor. On the stairway wall were paintings of whaling scenes. He continued his habit of long walks daily, whatever the weather. Later, he would take his granddaughters Eleanor and Frances to see the animals in the Central Park zoo, or rowing on the lake.

An apprentice at a bookshop where Melville bought "bundles of books" recalled him in later years as walking with a rapid stride, wearing a low-crowned hat and almost invariably a blue suit. Despite his reputation for being distant, or cold, Melville, he said, had a "gentle manner" and "pleasant smile."

At the end of November 1866, a great change occurred in Melville's life. He was appointed an inspector of customs for the port of New York. It came about through a chance meeting in Europe in 1856 with another traveler, Henry Smythe, collector of customs in New York. Smythe nominated his friend for the job, and the secretary of the treasury approved it. It would be the first regular income for Melville since he had come home from the seas twenty-two years ago.

Some Melville scholars believe Melville got the appointment at the New York Customs House because of his political essay attached to *Battle-Pieces*. Although there were a great many applicants for the patronage job, the administration gave Melville preference as the payoff for his support of President Johnson's conservative policy on Reconstruction.

The pay was $4 a day, for a six-day week, or $1,200 a year. During the nineteen years he would stay on the job, he never received a raise. For comparison, note that he could buy an apple for a penny, and a book for a dollar. About half of all industrial workers of that time made less than $500 a year.

Melville's job was to check docking certificates and bills of lading for all incoming ships, and to inspect cargoes for prohibited imports. In addition, he had to itemize all provisions before they were loaded onto outgoing ships.

Basically, this was administrative work. Year after year he had to fill out and file the same kinds of reports. Part of the time he was out on the docks, part of the time in an office. Like all political appointments, it was subject to the whims and prejudices of the higher-ups, a source of constant worry. But he quietly resisted the rampant bribery and corruption on the docks and built a reputation for honesty that kept his job safe.

Having a steady income did not create a happier family. It's hard to picture someone of his brilliance and talent confined to so routine a post for a good part of his life. That it could make him sad, angry, irritable, and depressed is no wonder. We know little about the inner life of their marriage.

One of Melville's biographers, Elizabeth Hardwick, wrote that he "was consumed by rage, breakdown, misery uncontrolled, given to violence in the household." Liz became desperate, fearing that Herman might really be going insane, as others had charged. Her Boston family urged her to leave him, but she decided not to.

Then, early one morning in September 1867 they found their son Malcolm in his bedroom, dead, with a bullet wound in his head. Family and friends, seeing suicide as a sin and a crime, refused to believe the coroner's verdict that it was suicide. As one of Malcolm's uncles said, he was beloved of everyone, and never suspected of having an evil thought. How could he have killed himself? It must have been an accident.

As was inevitable when reaching middle age, the Melvilles suffered other losses. Herman's brother Allan died in 1872, and his mother, Maria, a few months later. Life was made a bit easier, however, when his brother Tom, quitting the sea, was appointed governor of the Sailors' Snug Harbor, on

Staten Island. It was a home for aged, disabled, and destitute sailors. The salary was high, and the governor's mansion a comfortable gathering place for the family on holidays. Herman and his family enjoyed visits to Tom, but he couldn't forget that while he was stuck in a menial job, others in the family were well-to-do, or even rich.

He haunted bookshops in his spare time, wrote poems—at night, Sundays, holidays—studied art history and kept to himself. Liz, badly needing a break, took to spending summers away from him, leaving him, as he said, "decidedly lonely often in the house."

When an Authors Club was founded in the 1880s he refused an invitation to join, saying he "had become too much of a hermit" to mix with people.

In 1884, his brother Tom, fifty-five, died suddenly of a heart attack. Tom, not Herman, had long been the family's center, and Herman was in no condition to replace him. In 1885, on the last day of the year, Melville quit his customs job. He was now sixty-six and for some time heart disease had been gradually weakening him. Still, he continued to write poems, publishing two volumes, at his own expense. And he succeeded in creating a short novel, *Billy Budd: Sailor*. He was still trying to polish his last work in prose when he died. Liz stored the manuscript in a tin breadbox, where it was found after her death. But not until 1924 was it published, when interest in Melville's work was renewed.

Billy Budd is probably Melville's most familiar work today. It is the story of an innocent sailor, falsely accused of mutiny, who kills his accuser, and is condemned to death for it by the ship's captain. It is written in such a way that readers ardently debate what Melville meant by it. Is Billy's death the outcome of an absurd world? Or is it meant as a furious revolt against authority? However you interpret it, it has stimulated artists to re-create *Billy Budd* in drama, opera, and film.

*Herman and
Elizabeth in 1885,
the year Herman quit
his job of nineteen years
at the customs house.*

Melville died on September 28, 1891. There were few notices of his passing. One obituary said that "even his own generation has long thought him dead, so quiet have been the later years of his life." Yet there were some in his later years who continued to value his work. He was seen as one of the "writers of the deep." An editor chose some of his poems for an anthology. A British publisher asked him to write his reminiscences. But upon his death, interest died with him, until the Melville revival that began in the 1920s.

He was buried at Woodlawn Cemetery in the Bronx, next to his sons Malcolm and Stanwix.

We know now that Herman Melville was ahead of his time as a writer. Though his tragic symbolism and complex psychological themes did not appeal to the audience of his day, modern readers have found in his writings a wealth of meaning. So it was that in the decades following Melville's death, his genius was recognized—and he earned his rightful place among the great figures of American literature.

The Melville gravesite, with Elizabeth's grave next to Herman's.

Let the final word on Melville's achievement as an artist be his own. The poem by Melville most often found in anthologies is called "Art." In it he examines the creative process, seeing it as the mating of "unlike things," and comparing it to the struggle in the Old Testament between Jacob and the Angel. Scholars believe Melville began working on the poem in the 1870s. He reworked it many times, and various versions exist in draft form. It is like a sonnet, but with only eleven lines, not the traditional fourteen. This is the final form:

> In placid hours well pleased we dream
> Of many a brave unbodied scheme.
> But form to lend, pulsed life create,
> What unlike things must meet and mate;
> A flame to melt—a wind to freeze;
> Sad patience—joyous energies;
> Humility—yet pride and scorn;
> Instinct and study; love and hate;
> Audacity—reverence. These must mate,
> And fuse with Jacob's mystic heart,
> To wrestle with the angel—Art.

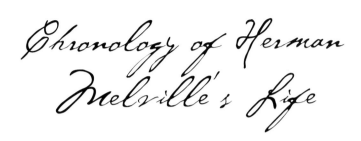

Chronology of Herman Melville's Life

1819	Born August 1, New York City, third child and second son of Allan Melvill and Maria Gansevoort Melvill
1825–1829	Attends New York Male High School
1830	Father in financial trouble. Family moves to Albany, New York Herman attends Albany Academy
1832	Allan Melvill dies. Maria adds "e" to family name
1833–1835	While at school, clerks part-time in bank and in brother's cap and fur store
1836	Much of year spent at Pittsfield, Massachusetts, farm of Uncle Thomas Melvill
1837–1838	Teaches school in Pittsfield. Family moves to Lansingburgh, New York, near Albany
1838–1839	Engineering student at Lansingburgh Academy
1839	From June to September serves as ordinary seaman on packet *St. Lawrence* on New York–Liverpool roundtrip Upon return teaches at academy in Greenbush, New York
1840	Teaches in spring in Brunswick, New York, then visits Uncle Thomas Melvill in Galena, Illinois. Goes to New Bedford, Massachusetts
1841	January 3 departs for Pacific aboard whaler *Acushnet*
1842–1844	Jumps ship in Marquesas; makes way to Tahiti, then Honolulu. Enlists on U.S. Navy frigate *United States*. Discharged in Boston, October 1844
1845	Writes *Typee*. Brother Gansevoort Melville, working in London, places book with British publisher
1846	Writes *Omoo*
1847	Marries Elizabeth Shaw of Boston. They will have four children. Moves to Manhattan

1848	Writes *Mardi*
1849	Writes *Redburn* and *White-Jacket*. Voyages to England and France
1850	Writes *Moby-Dick*. Meets Nathaniel Hawthorne. Moves to farmhouse in Pittsfield, Massachusetts
1853–1854	His stories appear in *Putnam's* and *Harper's* magazines
1855	Publishes *Israel Potter*
1856	Publishes *The Piazza Tales*. Travels in Europe, Egypt, and Palestine
1857	Publishes *The Confidence-Man*. Begins three-year lecture series
1860	Sails to San Francisco on clipper ship *Meteor*
1863	Moves from Pittsfield to New York
1864	Visits Civil War battlefields
1866	Harper's Brothers publishes Civil War poems, *Battle-Pieces*. Takes up job in New York Customs House
1876	Privately publishes *Clarel*, poem about pilgrimage to Holy Land
1885	Retires from Customs House
1888	Privately publishes poems: *John Marr and Other Sailors*
1891	Privately publishes *Timoleon*, a book of poems. Works on *Billy Budd*. Dies September 28. Buried in Woodlawn Cemetery, Bronx, New York
1924	First publication of *Billy Budd* and other late writings

Bibliography

MELVILLE'S BOOKS

The Battle-Pieces of Herman Melville. Edited with an introduction and notes by Hennig Cohen. New York: Thomas Yoseloff, 1964.

Billy Budd, Sailor (An Inside Narrative Reading Text and Genetic Text). Edited by Harrison Hayford and Merton Sealts Jr. Chicago: University of Chicago Press, 1962.

Clarel: A Poem and Pilgrimage in the Holy Land. Edited by Harrison Hayford, Hershel Parker, and G. Thomas Tanselle. Evanston and Chicago: Northwestern University Press and the Newberry Library, 1991.

Collected Poems of Herman Melville. Edited by Howard P. Vincent. Chicago: Packard and Co., Hendricks House, 1947.

The Confidence-Man: His Masquerade. Edited by Harrison Hayford, Hershel Parker, and G. Thomas Tanselle. Evanston and Chicago: Northwestern University Press and the Newberry Library, 1984.

Correspondence. Edited by Lynn Horth. Evanston and Chicago: Northwestern University Press and the Newberry Library, 1993.

Israel Potter: His Fifty Years in Exile. Edited by Harrison Hayford, Hershel Parker, and G. Thomas Tanselle. Evanston and Chicago: Northwestern University Press and the Newberry Library, 1982.

Journals. Edited by Howard Horsford and Lynn Horth. Evanston and Chicago: Northwestern University Press and the Newberry Library, 1989.

The Letters of Herman Melville. Edited by Merrell R. Davis and William H. Gilman. New Haven: Yale University Press, 1960.

Mardi and the Voyage Thither. Edited by Harrison Hayford, Hershel Parker, and G. Thomas Tanselle. Evanston and Chicago: Northwestern University Press and the Newberry Library, 1970.

Melville's Marginalia. Edited by Walker Cowan. New York: Garland, 1987.

Moby-Dick, or The Whale. Edited by Harrison Hayford, Hershel Parker, and G. Thomas Tanselle. Evanston and Chicago: Northwestern University Press and the Newberry Library, 1988.

Moby-Dick, or The Whale. The Northwestern-Newberry text, with introduction by Andrew Delbanco, notes and explanatory commentary by Tom Quirk. New York: Penguin Books, 1992.

Omoo: A Narrative of Adventures in the South Seas. Edited by Harrison Hayford, Hershel Parker, and G. Thomas Tanselle. Evanston and Chicago: Northwestern University Press and the Newberry Library, 1968.

Piazza Tales and Other Prose Pieces 1839–1860. Edited by Harrison Hayford, Alma MacDougall, and G. Thomas Tanselle. Evanston and Chicago: Northwestern University Press and the Newberry Library, 1987.

Pierre, or The Ambiguities. Edited by Harrison Hayford, Hershel Parker, and G. Thomas Tanselle. Evanston and Chicago: Northwestern University Press and the Newberry Library, 1971.

Redburn: His First Voyage, Being the Sailor-boy Confessions and Reminiscences of the Son-of-a-Gentleman, in the Merchant Service. Edited by Harrison Hayford, Hershel Parker, and G. Thomas Tanselle. Evanston and Chicago: Northwestern University Press and the Newberry Library, 1969.

Typee: A Peep at Polynesian Life. Edited by Harrison Hayford, Hershel Parker, and G. Thomas Tanselle. Evanston and Chicago: Northwestern University Press and the Newberry Library, 1968.

Weeds and Wildings Chiefly: with a Rose or Two. Reading Text and Genetic Text. Edited and with an introduction by Robert Charles Ryan. Evanston, IL: Northwestern University Press, 1967.

White-Jacket, or The World in a Man-of-War. Edited by Harrison Hayford, Hershel Parker, and G. Thomas Tanselle. Evanston and Chicago: Northwestern University Press and the Newberry Library, 1970.

For Further Reading

The standard and most detailed biography of Melville is in two volumes by Hershel Parker. *Herman Melville: A Biography, Volume 1, 1819–1851,* and *Volume 2, 1852–1891.* Baltimore and London: The Johns Hopkins University Press, 1996 and 2002. I am grateful for the depth and breadth of his work.

Hardwick, Elizabeth. *Herman Melville.* New York: Viking Penguin, 2000.

Karcher, Carolyn L. *Shadow Over the Promised Land: Slavery, Race and Violence in Melville's America.* Baton Rouge: Louisiana University Press, 1980.

Levine, Robert S., ed. *Cambridge Companion to Herman Melville.* New York: Cambridge University Press, 1998.

Leyda, Jay, ed. *The Indispensable Melville.* New York: The Book Society, 1952.

Mayoux, Jean-Jacques. *Melville.* New York: Evergreen, 1960.

Miller, Perry. *The Raven and the Whale.* New York: Harcourt Brace, 1956.

Philbrick, Nathaniel. *In the Heart of the Sea: The Tragedy of the Whaleship Essex.* New York: Viking, 2000.

Robertson-Lorant, Laurie. *Melville: A Biography.* New York: Clarkson Potter, 1996.

Rollyson, Carl, and Lisa Paddock. *Herman Melville: A to Z.* New York: Checkmark Books, 2001.

Selby, Nick, ed. *Herman Melville: Moby-Dick.* New York: Columbia University Press, 1998.

A great many editions of Melville's prose and poetry have been published. Many of *Moby-Dick* are available, some very inexpensive. Paperback collections of the shorter works include *Billy Budd and Other Tales* (introduction by Joyce Carol Oates), New York: Signet, 1998; *Great Short Works of Herman Melville* (editor, Warner Berthoff), New York: Harper Perennial, 1969; *Herman Melville, The Complete Shorter Fiction* (introduction by John Updike), Chicago: Everyman's Library, 1997; and *Herman Melville: Tales, Poems and Other Writings* (edited by John Bryant), New York: Modern Library, 2002.

Visiting Herman Melville Sites

Arrowhead: Home of Herman Melville. 780 Holmes Road, Pittsfield, MA 01201. Tel. (413) 442-1793. House tours, nature trail, museum shop. Open daily May–Oct. 31, 9:30–5.

Herman Melville House (Lansingburgh Historical Society). 2 114th Street (P.O. Box 219, Lansingburgh Station), Troy, NY 12182. Tel. (518) 235-3501. Open by appointment. Artifacts and books relating to Melville and Lansingburgh. Melville Park (adjacent) on Hudson River is the site of a shipyard active during Melville's residency.

Herman Melville Memorial Room, Berkshire Athenaeum, 1 Wendell Avenue, Pittsfield, MA. 01201. Large collection of Melville family books, pictures, letters, and memorabilia. Mon.–Sat., 9–5.

Whaling Museum, 13 Broad St., Nantucket, MA. Contains collection of whaling memorabilia, portraits, paintings, and scrimshaw. Illustrates how whales were harpooned and processed for their oil while at sea. Rare artifacts from the *Essex,* ship rammed by sperm whale, an event that inspired the novel *Moby-Dick*. Hours: May 25–Oct. 14, Mon.–Sat., 10–5, Sun., 12–5. Tel. (508) 228-1894.

New Bedford Whaling Museum, 19 Johnny Cake Hill, New Bedford, MA. 02740-6398. Hours: daily 9–5. Tel. (508) 997-0046.

Web Sites on Herman Melville:
http://www.melville.org
http://www.keele.ac.uk/depts/as literature
Moby-Dick/am/amlist.whale-pages.html

Index

Page numbers in *italic* indicate photographs or illustrations.

About The Author

Milton Meltzer's biographies of American writers include Walt Whitman, Carl Sandburg, Edgar Allan Poe, Langston Hughes, Mark Twain, and now Herman Melville. He has written more than one hundred books for young people and adults and has written and edited for newspapers, magazines, radio, television, and films.

Five of his books have been finalists for the National Book Award. In 2001 he was the recipient of the Laura Ingalls Wilder Award, given by the American Library Association for lifetime achievement in children's literature. Many of his books have been chosen for the honor lists of the National Council of Teachers of English, the National Council for the Social Studies, the New York Public Library's annual Books for the Teen Age, and The New York Times Best Books of the Year list.

Born in Worcester, Massachusetts, Mr. Meltzer was educated at Columbia University. He is a member of the Authors Guild, American PEN, and the Organization of American Historians. He and his wife live in New York City.